"*Aggressively Happy*: a book one s
to find, where the writer speaks you
but even more satisfying is when a book reads me. That's one
of the ways I'm reassured I am not alone.

Clarkson: part poet, stirred by choice classics, powerful
quotes, and Sacred Writ, which I find an irresistible combination in a writer's ink. Come, pour a cup of tea, and let's perk
up with joy!"

Patsy Clairmont, author, artist, creativity coach

"Trouble will find you, but joy must be sought out. That's the
premise of Joy Clarkson's honest and hopeful book. It is not a
pep talk, not a denial of sorrow, and not a set of techniques to
paper over the pain. Instead, with lyrical prose and delightful
storytelling, she draws you in, like friends talking over a cup of
tea, and imparts a wealth of insight from Scripture, theology,
poetry, and the saints. This is a rich and holistic vision that
will provide not only the fertilizer but also the practices and
the tools for cultivating a sturdy kind of joy."

Rev. Dr. Glenn Packiam, associate senior pastor of New Life
Church and author of *The Resilient Pastor*
and *Blessed Broken Given*

"Joy Clarkson is the pen pal you need in your life. This intimate,
welcoming book is full of unpretentious wisdom about our life
in and with God. I read it and thought, *For once! An enjoyable
book that is edifying, and an edifying book that is actually
enjoyable!* Read this book with friends. Read this book with
an embarrassingly large cup of hot chocolate or tea. Read this
book under a blanket by a window while it rains outside. The
main thing is to read *Aggressively Happy*!"

Michael Wear, author of *Reclaiming Hope: Lessons Learned in
the Obama White House About the Future of Faith in America*

"Joy Clarkson is a fearless and formidable advocate for delight in an age of rage and distraction. Her unflappable hope and sense of enchantment radiate through every page of *Aggressively Happy*, where she champions faith, defies the cynics, and even redeems one of literature's most misunderstood characters."

Boze Herrington, novelist

"This is not a book that feels like a chat over coffee with a chum. This is a book that feels like a sumptuous feast in a castle with your long-lost best friend. Savor this magical book and carry its wisdom with you as you face life's storms."

Haley Stewart, author of *The Grace of Enough* and *Jane Austen's Genius Guide to Life*

"In *Aggressively Happy*, Joy reminds us that happiness is not a saccharine sentiment; in a world drawn to despair, 'the joy of the Lord is our strength.' This book rings with beauty and truth and will help readers develop a practice of joy that can endure hardship and suffering."

Grace Olmstead, author of *Uprooted: Recovering the Legacy of the Places We've Left Behind*

"Is it possible to be thoroughly happy while also accepting the difficulties that life inevitably brings? Joy Clarkson answers a remarkable and resounding yes, an answer that includes such things as *Pride and Prejudice*, scones, *Harry Potter*, agonized doubts, Korean boy bands, and—most importantly—the Gospels."

Dr. Holly Ordway

aggressively
happy

aggressively happy

A Realist's Guide to Believing in the Goodness of Life

JOY MARIE CLARKSON

BETHANYHOUSE

a division of Baker Publishing Group
Minneapolis, Minnesota

© 2022 by Joy Marie Clarkson

Published by Bethany House Publishers
11400 Hampshire Avenue South
Minneapolis, Minnesota 55438
www.bethanyhouse.com

Bethany House Publishers is a division of
Baker Publishing Group, Grand Rapids, Michigan

Printed in the United States of America

Library of Congress Cataloging-in-Publication Data
Names: Clarkson, Joy, author.
Title: Aggressively happy : a realist's guide to believing in the goodness of life / Joy Marie Clarkson.
Description: Minneapolis, Minnesota : Bethany House Publishers, a division of Baker Publishing Group, [2022]
Identifiers: LCCN 2021043346 | ISBN 9780764238246 (paperback) | ISBN 9780764240553 (casebound) | ISBN 9781493435944 (ebook)
Subjects: LCSH: Joy—Religious aspects—Christianity. | Happiness—Religious aspects—Christianity.
Classification: LCC BV4647.J68 C53 2022 | DDC 241/.4—dc23
LC record available at https://lccn.loc.gov/2021043346

Cover design by Kathleen Lynch / Black Kat Design
Cover image © Ashraful Arefin / Trevillion Images

Published in association with The Bindery Agency, TheBinderyAgency.com

Baker Publishing Group publications use paper produced from sustainable forestry practices and post-consumer waste whenever possible.

22 23 24 25 26 27 28   7 6 5 4 3 2 1

To Lilian Joy,
who makes me aggressively happy

Be joyful though you have considered all the facts.

Wendell Berry, "Manifesto:
The Mad Farmer Liberation Front"

Whatever happens, my dear brothers and sisters,
rejoice in the Lord. I never get tired of telling you
these things, and I do it to safeguard your faith.

Philippians 3:1 NLT

contents

introduction

Decide to live

There are a thousand thousand reasons to live this life, every one of them sufficient.

—Marilynne Robinson, *Gilead*

It was December 31, 6:45 a.m. My roommate was still fast asleep, the covers pulled just over her head rising and falling to the rhythm of her deep breaths. I sat in my bed with a warm cup of tea, a candle lit, utterly happy. I have always loved the stillness before the world is awake, when there is silence enough to hear the murmurs of your own hopes and desires more clearly. That morning I had a purpose: to prepare for the new year. As I sipped my tea, I perused the past year in my mind like I was flipping through a picture book, treasuring all the good things, the happy memories I had made, moments of growth. There had been difficulties, yes, but they seemed so outweighed by goodness. As my mug radiated heat through my fingertips, my heart warmed with gratitude. I felt a deep, palpable peace. From this stillness, a message came to my heart.

This year will be hard. You will suffer. The people you love will suffer. Prepare yourself.

I paused and opened my eyes. *That is probably the general anxiety disorder speaking,* I thought. I am accustomed to a persistent sense of impending doom and to intrusive images of all the things that could go wrong, from broken plates to missent emails, to crushed limbs, to global nuclear catastrophe. All in a day's dread! I read an article recently that found that a large portion of adults diagnosed with anxiety, depression, and OCD are of Scotch-Irish heritage. Perhaps it was centuries of rain pelting sardonic gloom into our genetic code, or a history of familial conflict with our self-righteous brother, England. Whatever the reason, the Clarksons have not bucked the trend. My dad's side came from Edinburgh, and my mom's from Belfast. If God had wanted to make us serene, God could have made us Finnish! (Finland has repeatedly won the "most happy country in the world" award.) I've often prepared a small speech in my mind for my future spouse about the high likelihood of our children inheriting mental illness: *Dear, I'm bringing great hair, bad knees, and clinical depression to the table.* But would Yeats, Heaney, and Hopkins have written such beautiful poetry if they hadn't been so sad? Despite very little sign of a blossoming career in poetry, I comfort myself with these thoughts.

So my first inclination was to call the doom-and-gloom voice in my head an intrusive thought, have a bite of something with protein in it, do some breathing exercises, and carry on reveling in the nearly perfect morning. Slightly agitated, I closed my eyes, attempting to reclaim tranquility. But the message came again, as clear as if my roommate had emerged from her cocoon of slumber to dictate the message herself:

This year will be hard. You will suffer. The people you love will suffer. Prepare yourself.

It was like I'd paused a song, which now resumed at a slightly louder volume. I shook my head again, hoping the thought might trickle out my left ear like a tablespoon of presumptuous pool water from the college gym. But with one last burst of urgency, I felt it to be undeniably true.

The year would be hard. I would suffer. I needed to be prepared.

This time I listened. I knew in my gut that this was not the voice of fear or anxiety. It was not angry; I was not being punished. It was the voice of my mom calling me to let me know there's traffic ahead, and to leave a little early. It was the voice of a friend tipping me off to the high expectations of a difficult professor. It was the voice of a doctor, about to draw blood, two seconds before the needle went in.

Quiet Desperation

I didn't tell anyone about my omen. I'm really not one for direct messages from God. I have, from time to time, wished to hear an audible voice from heaven announcing definitively that God exists, or telling me who to marry or where to go to grad school. But, alas! I am subject, like most other people, to the vagaries of prayer, of belief, of faith. Truth be told, I have often doubted those who seem to have God's private phone number. It just doesn't seem realistic to say God told you where to park, and I think it would be better to tell the boy you're just not that into him rather than that God told you to break up with him (now you've heaped both divine *and* romantic disapproval on him, poor lad). For me, prayer is usually more about clearing away the clamor of life and the urgency of my insecurities so I can hear the steady, calm voice of wisdom humming beneath it all. That is why this experience was so strange. It had a conspiracy theorist–street preacher vibe to it. I felt almost embarrassed. And when I didn't feel embarrassed, I felt annoyed. For twenty-odd years my call had gone to voicemail, and all at once I got a message from an unlisted number with a foreboding voice at the other end telling me I was going to suffer.

So, I told no one and went about my business, quietly waiting for the shoe to drop. And it did.

It dishonors a sorrow to tell it to too many people, I think, and it was not entirely my own sorrow to tell, so I hope you will excuse me if I do not share the particulars here. It is enough to say that it was crushing, that it went on and on, that there could be no happy ending. And yet, with the great grief of it clawing for my total attention, I somehow managed to graduate from college, get into Oxford and Yale for courses in religion and literature, and to turn them both down. I had tried and tried to talk myself into saying yes to one of the opportunities—but I could not. The more I prayed about it, and sought that quiet voice, the more it evaded me. I could not be at peace about them, so I turned them down, half-convinced it was what God wanted me to do and half-convinced I was insane for turning down the best opportunities I might ever have.

More than anything, I was just bone tired. When I was honest with myself, I feared, as fragile as I was, that if I had gone,

I would have splintered, leaked, and failed. I see now that there was a wisdom in my hesitancy, but at the time all I could feel was that I was stupid for turning down two dream opportunities. I felt that I was a coward or a fool, or very possibly both. I moved home to work and save money and get my bearings. I was so exhausted from the disappointment and sadness of it all that I was barely able to be pleasant. I began to feel that I was a drain to everyone around me. Not that there were many people around me, because I was in that strange position of returning to a place where you had once been a very different person and feeling oddly disjointed from the people you knew in high school. I avoided the friends I did have because they acted so awkward around me, either conspicuously avoiding any discussion of the Sad Thing while indicating its presence with a dozen significant looks, or trying to shore up the open-ended pain of it with well-meaning words. For the first time in my life, I thought a lot about dying. I didn't want to die, exactly. I was just tired of living, tired of being in pain, tired of feeling lost, tired of being a drain to the people around me.

So I threw myself into a handful of unglamorous jobs and tried to be okay. Henry David Thoreau aptly wrote that "the mass of men live lives of quiet desperation,"[1] and I was quietly desperate. I grew to hate the silence of early mornings. With nothing to distract me, my sadness and my failures would visit me. I tried to avoid their gazes, but when there was no one else in the room, I couldn't help but acknowledge their persistent presence, their unflinching glares. The quiet mornings that were once a balm to my soul now felt like a poorly fitting shoe chafing a raw blister, opening an old wound again and again.

One of my unglamorous jobs was working at a local coffee shop. I enjoyed the intense physicality of this job and the constant social interaction, which helpfully distracted me and kept me from wallowing. One morning, I rolled out of bed at 5:30 a.m. to open the shop. The temperature had fallen below zero, and I shivered as I clumsily unlocked the door to my car. It groaned in indignation as I sat down, and sputtered into life resentfully as I turned the keys. I plugged in my iPhone and put a playlist on shuffle, hoping some female folk music would wake me up gently.

As I turned out of my neighborhood, I thought of that December morning almost a year before. Jealousy, yes it was jealousy, of my past self for having access to such uncomplicated happiness and peace seized my chest. I felt like I had been a better person before, and sorrow had made something small and brittle of me. My own face seemed oddly unfamiliar as I caught sight of my care-weary eyes in the rearview mirror. Who was that? Could she ever be happy again? Feel lightness?

As I crested a hill, a mountain vista greeted me, beckoning my eyes away from the rearview mirror. The silhouettes of the peaks loomed immense in the azure sky. A hint of pink, so faint it almost seemed like wishful thinking, peered over the mountains and breathed purple into the horizon. I felt thankful for a moment that even if I was miserable, the world went on being beautiful.

Suddenly, the final line of the chorus (and title of the song) I was listening to caught my ears: "You are here."[2] Somehow, it shifted something in me. I had been trying to escape the blunt reality of what my life was, afraid some deep despair would set in if I stopped fighting. I was exhausting myself wishing life was other than what it was. Suddenly, I realized: I was *here*. It was no good wishing I was someone else, somewhere else. And maybe that was okay.

When I arrived at the coffee shop, I left my car running and watched as the sun cast its rays on the mountainside. The rose hues of morning were no longer bashful but bold, illuminating the mountain, splashing each cloud with technicolor confidence. Millions of particles of frost sparkled on the asphalt of the parking lot in mundane glory. I listened to the song again.

When something, a song or a sunrise, pierces you straight to the heart, it's hard to put it into words. Perhaps this is why the great prophets in holy texts always sound so frantic trying to explain their spiritual experiences. "It was like a bird! It was on fire! The smoke filled the whole temple, which was also the universe!" Sometimes, moments of transcendent beauty can effect a transformation so complete that we're left bereft of words. We know something has changed, but how can we explain it? Without it sounding smaller and somehow less wonderful than it was?

But I will try.

Something in the alchemy of the sunrise and the gently chiding lyrics began a new thing in me. It wasn't a life lesson or a piece of great advice; it was a realization, an epiphany: this is life, the beauty and the pain together. A glorious sunrise coexistent with deep emotional pain, the utter brokenness of the world. One doesn't make the other untrue. This is always the bargain. If you get one, you get the other. And in that realization, I was offered a choice: Can you say yes to this? To life as it is? Will you live this beautiful, painful life?

> Can you say yes to this? To life as it is? Will you live this beautiful, painful life?

That day, I decided to live. I mean this in two ways. The first is that I stopped thinking about dying. I decided that whatever came, it was my job to see this one strange and wonderful life through to the very end. Where I once cherished a jealousy of my idealized past self, I began to develop a healthy amount of FOMO (Fear of Missing Out) on my future life. I began to think of all the sunrises I hadn't seen, all the huevos rancheros I hadn't eaten, the hands I hadn't held, the work I hadn't done. When I think back on it now, I feel an almost wild relief. I wish I could take my past self, hold her face in my hands, and tell her all the wonderful things I would have missed if I'd given up on life: the birth of my first niece (named for me—Lilian Joy), moving to Scotland, falling in love with a good man, making some of the best friendships of my life, discovering the immense gratification of bread baking and Dutch ovens, getting to teach bright-eyed freshmen, and many, many sunsets.

Choosing to Live

But it wasn't merely that I chose not to die—I chose to live. It is possible to choose not to die, and still not to live. I think that is where the quiet desperation comes from, a halfhearted acquiescence to existence, which resents the whole ordeal of living too much to care about sunrises, huevos rancheros, or romance. It is the heart weary of breaking that chooses instead not to care. And if I'm honest, it is this kind of living that has proven the hardest for me. It is hard to live with skin in the game, to feel the cold. Accepting the full breadth of both the deep pleasure and deep pain of life can seem like too much for a heart to bear.

18

But that day, I acknowledged a hunger for something deeper. If I was going to be alive in the world, I wanted to drink deep of goodness. I wanted life to mean something. I wanted to be honest and open, and if there was something true and beautiful in this world, I wanted to know what it was, and to live in its light. I began to hold on to life with white knuckles and to say, like Jacob, that ancient wrestler with God and man, "I will not let you go unless you bless me" (Genesis 32:26).

Is it too much to ask for blessing in this world? For happiness?

In the Sermon on the Mount, Jesus makes a list of "blessed" people. The Greek word used here is μακάριος, which could also accurately be translated as "happy" or "lucky," and is usually used of people who should be envied for their good fortune, wealth, or status in life. I've often heard people try to make some kind of distinction between happiness and joy, but Jesus makes no such distinction here. It is just plain old happy, lucky, satisfied, blessed.

These are the people Jesus calls happy:

The poor in spirit,
Those who mourn,
The meek,
Those who hunger and thirst for righteousness,
The merciful,
The pure in heart,
The peacemakers,
The persecuted,
The insulted and falsely accused (Matthew 5:3–11).

The blessed ones, the happy ones, are not people born to easy circumstances or with a sunny disposition. They are not people who simply "look on the bright side." They are hungry, thirsty, sad, and yet somehow blessed. The happiness they have persists beneath the weight of living, even blossoms defiantly out of it. It seemed to me that these happy and blessed people were the opposite of shallow, sheeny positivity. They've seen the heart of reality, and it is good. It is blessed. Happy.

Whatever they had, I wanted it.

When New Year's came around again that year, I began to re-assess the message I'd heard so clearly the previous year. I began to think that perhaps it wasn't an omen or a premonition; it was simply true. It was the steady, calm voice of wisdom: Life will be hard. You and the people you love will suffer. Be prepared.

But now I realized there was another truth: there will also be sunrises.

Aggressively Happy

This is a book about happiness. A long time ago, I had tweeted about something, probably tea or lipstick or something, when someone replied in the following way:

"This is disgusting. You are so aggressively happy."

I pondered this response for a moment, perplexed. But the more I thought about it, the more I liked it. To find a sturdy center of joy in this world takes a lot of work. I'm not always aggressively happy, but I want to be. So I thanked the disgruntled tweeter and added it to my bio.

Ever since then, I've thought of "Aggressively Happy" as a motto and identity.

And maybe after reading this book, you will too.

But perhaps, like the tweeter, you have mixed feelings about the idea of being "Aggressively Happy." You might find it annoying, like someone bursting into your room at 8 a.m., throwing open your blinds, and singing "Oh what a beautiful morning!" before shoving a cup of coffee into your hand (that you immediately spill) and asking if you're excited to embark on today's adventure, i.e., another day of work or school. On the face of it, there's nothing evil about this action. And yet, like any rational human being, you'd love nothing better than to pitch the life-adventure, coffee-bearing songbird out the open window and shout "bah humbug!" while you're doing it. It reminds me of a related verse in the Bible: "A loud and cheerful greeting early in the morning will be taken as a curse!" (Proverbs 27:14 NLT). Happiness is okay, but at the right volume, and not on weekday mornings.

Or you might feel a general haze of guilt around the idea of being happy. It may seem criminally insensitive to pursue joy when confronted with the deep sorrow, injustice, and chaos of the world. Happiness seems either willfully ignorant, in a state of denial, or callous to the pain of other people. To this way of thinking, the only acceptable mode of existence is either perpetual indignation or sympathetic depression. Or you might have a vague sense that desiring to be happy is too worldly. Kicking around in your subconscious is something about joy being different from happiness, and a general feeling that deep and holy people are serious and somber. You'd rather be aggressively holy than happy, and you're pretty sure you can't be both.

Maybe you're just cynical and think that happiness is an illusion, a benighted young philosopher taking a long drag on his cigarillo, thumping his copy of *The Stranger* and muttering, "Life is pain." Each passing year of chaos reinforces your suspicions that all happiness in this world is an abnormality, maybe even a defect. You think that if anyone really had a handle on the world, they'd be knowing, tragic, and cynical. Happiness is either unrealistic ignorance or an insincere performance for some nefarious reason. Nothing personal. You just don't believe in it. If you see yourself in one of these descriptions, I want you to know that this book is for you. It's for you because I have felt each of these things, sometimes even still *feel* these things deep in my bones, but I've come to believe there are other, better ways to live.

Perhaps it will help if I clarify what this book is *not* about. It is not about being happy *all the time*. There is such a thing as toxic positivity, a compulsive need to look on the bright side that lends itself to a perpetual denial of the real, deep difficulties of life. A happiness that ignores pain, injustice, and brokenness is not worth having. But a happiness that can stand tall, look life in the eye, and smile anyway? That is well worth the fight. And a fight it must be. Patching together a joyful life takes far more effort than submitting to the soporific lull of cynicism. Cultivating happiness takes grit, determination, and a good sense of humor. It's a lot of work.

So why should you do it?

I can think of three reasons.

The first is that life will be more pleasant for you. Here's the thing: life is hard. No matter who is president or how much you trust God or how far ahead you plan or how beautiful you are. Life is hard. Marriages end. Viruses sweep across the globe, ending lives and livelihoods. Life is hard on the outside, in all the crazy things that happen to us and our society. But life is also hard on the inside, where we carry loneliness no lover can fix, where abuse has left its scars.

If we accept that life will be full of difficulties and sorrows, we then have two options: to resign ourselves to life generally being a bummer, or to seek enjoyment, delight, and hope in the midst of (and in spite of!) life's ups and downs. To put it bluntly: you could choose to cultivate happiness or you could not. If it is possible to be blessed, I think we should go for it.

The second is that life will be more pleasant for people around you. I want you to know something: you affect the people around you. When you cultivate a perspective on life that is joyful and life-giving, it spills out into the lives of others. Far from being insensitive or unrealistic, cultivating a life of joy that nourishes others is one of the most generous and practical things you could do to make the world a better place. And your joy will grow as a result of seeing the fruits of your bravery in other people's lives. It is the opposite of a vicious circle.

Are you determined to add to the noxious emissions of depression and cynicism? Well, knock yourself out, I suppose. But I wish you wouldn't. And guess what? You don't have to.

The final and most important reason to cultivate happiness is that happiness tells the truth about the world. Let me lay my cards on the table: I have come to believe there is a deep well of happiness at the heart of life. I believe that for all of its darkness, and mundanity, and confusion, life is good, and was made to be

> Cultivating a life of joy that nourishes others is one of the most generous and practical things you could do to make the world a better place.

good, deep down to its core. I believe being alive is a precious gift, and the greatest crime is to squander it. I believe that there's reason to hope. I know I can't exactly prove these things, but in my experience, life is better when you live like they're true.

This book is about learning to live like it's true.

It's been five years since I decided to live. My journey of Aggressive Happiness is just beginning, but I want to invite you to join me. I think the world needs more aggressively happy people, people whose whole will is bent on finding the loveliness of life and giving themselves as a gift to a weary and cynical world. But before you set out on your way, let me tell you how to read this book.

I've organized this book around ten verbs:

Befriend sadness.

Flounder well.

Remember: you have a body!

Enjoy things unironically.

Tell yourself a good story.

Be like Mr. Collins.

Believe in God.

Accept love.

Expect the end of the world.

Give yourself away.

I think of these as my rules for living a happy life. I have tried to arrange these in a thematically helpful way, but they do not need to be read in order. They each contain stories from many different periods in my life, along with poems, songs, saints, and ideas that have put wind in my sails and hope in my heart.

Which relates to one other thing—at the end of each chapter I've included three suggestions: something to read, something to see, and something to listen to. Art, poetry, and music help me make sense of life, and so I chose to include art that has helped me live an aggressively happy life. You can find most of the suggested artwork/poetry/pieces of music online for free. I hope they will help you not only think but feel your way through the ideas in this book, and that they will bring some joy, beauty, and poignancy into your days. I have also included some things to ponder as you spend time with these works of art.

I do not claim to know the whole story yet; I am a novice in this blessed life. But in this book, I have tried to pass on some of the lessons I have learned, in hope that they might help other people along their own paths. Most of all, I hope this book makes you aggressively happy every time you read it. I hope each chapter will make you laugh, maybe even cry (an author can dream!), and leave you feeling like life is a little more possible.

And then I hope you will put down the book and go live an aggressively happy life.

1

Befriend sadness

While we are in this life, [we] have in ourselves a marvellous mixture of both happiness and sorrow. . . . We remain in this mixed state all the days of our life. But [Christ] wants us to trust that he is perpetually with us.

—Julian of Norwich, *Revelations of Divine Love*

The air was so humid you could taste it. Little clouds of bugs wafted through the golden evening light, looking almost beautiful when the sun caught them just so. It was a little too warm to be bracing, but something like invigoration thumped through my veins. It was my first week at college, and everything was wonderfully new and exciting. It may have only been a private Christian college in Southern California, but to me it felt like the Amazon, the Alps, or the deep blue sea: unknown terrain, full of exciting things for me, the intrepid adventurer, to experience. The world was my oyster, and I was quite at my leisure.

I was on my way to the first meeting of a club I was considering joining. Interested freshmen were directed to meet on the soccer field near the old middle school. This was an oddity of attending school in California; you could always count on the weather being uncomfortably warm but not prohibitively unpleasant, and so student groups often met outside rather than go to the trouble of reserving a room. As I approached the appointed field, I spied a small crowd of shy-looking freshmen mulling around awkwardly and introducing themselves to one another, and a smaller group of smug-looking sophomores telling inside jokes. They were infinitely superior to us, of course, because they already had established social groups.

There was one particularly smug-looking sophomore strutting around like he was the king of the jungle. And for all I knew, he was. He had a full head of golden curls, which he held at a quizzical angle and through which he periodically ran his fingers. He was prowling around, like a big cat on the lookout for a juicy wildebeest to eat.

When I arrived at the welcome table, a kind and decidedly not smug-looking girl greeted me and directed me to a pile of name tags and markers. I plucked up a deep-purple pen from the pile and wrote my name in big swirling letters: "Joy."

I added a heart. Pleased with my work, I affixed the name tag to my chest and sought to ingratiate myself to some of the other newbs. I found a group of pleasant-looking people sitting under a tree and joined them, tucking my legs comfortably under myself and enjoying the plush carpet of grass. To my surprise, after a few minutes of ritual college conversation with my fellow freshmen ("What's your name? Where are you from? What are you majoring in? Which dorm do you live in?"), I saw the King of the Jungle approaching. He sat down next to me in a way that suggested I should be honored by this condescension. He stretched out on the lawn and proceeded to rip up the grass and absentmindedly deposit it in a little pile, stopping occasionally to tousle his curls. After a few minutes of lazily shouting at his friend across the circle, his attention shifted toward me. He shamelessly ogled my name tag.

Joy Marie

"So," he said, making eye contact in an unnerving way, "your name is Joy."

I nodded to indicate that this was, in fact, the case.

"So, do you feel like you always have to be happy? Like you can never be sad?"

This was intended to be a piercing question, but it was not exactly novel. I am used to people making puns with my name, bursting into song ("Joy, Joy, Joy, Joy down in my heart . . . WHERE?!"), or commenting that I "suit my name" with a generic reference to my cheerful disposition. Every once in a while, my name awakens some hovering existential quandary regarding the nature of happiness, causing people to ask questions like the King of the Jungle just had. When strangers ask such probing questions, I am often tempted to reply, "I don't know, Stacey. That seems a little personal. How's your marriage?" But I usually don't. I usually just laugh and comment on the hors d'oeuvres. But this time something impish got into me, and I couldn't resist.

"Well, actually," I said with a smile, "my full name is Joy Marie."

He looked unmoved, like this didn't change things. I went on. "Marie means 'sea of bitterness' or 'sea of sorrow.' So, I like to think of my name as a motto more than a description. 'Joy in the sea of bitterness.'"

His eyes began to glaze over.

"Life is full of bitterness, don't you think? But it is possible to make it through on a boat of joy. The whole ocean can't drown a tiny boat as long as the water doesn't get inside."

This was more than the King of the Jungle had bargained for. He was not enjoying himself. He nodded vacantly and shifted his attention to another innocent freshman, to whom he no doubt asked invasive questions. I grinned and sought a new conversation partner. I did not join the club.

The Contradictions of Joy Marie

My mother would swear on a Bible that Marie means "wished-for child." While I fully embrace this maternal affirmation of my existence, I have always preferred the paradoxical interpretation of my name. She had me when she was forty-two, after three miscarriages. Not knowing my sex, during her pregnancy, my mother's friends would always pray for "Baby Joy." I can't help but see a little narrative continuity in the name. I was born when I shouldn't have been, a joy in a sea of sorrow. But it's more than that. I hold on to it because it expresses something I have always felt to be fundamentally true about myself.

Let me explain.

JOY.

I have sometimes privately wondered if I enjoyed life more than the average person.

I love being alive. On days when all is well, I wake up with a sense of secret delight, a canary in my pocket that sings its heart out even if only I can hear. I take immense pleasure in all the small things of life: a warm mug of tea as sunshine creeps through my curtains, my golden bullet of love (i.e., the family dog, Darcy), a fresh blank page waiting to be scribbled on. When I step outside on a spring day and breathe deep of the wet wondrousness of new life welling up in every blooming corner of creation, I can't imagine what we did to deserve this world so full of wonders. Music is a physical thing with me; it is color and emotion seeping into every corner of my being. Sometimes when I listen to Dvorak, I'm surprised light doesn't come out my fingertips. I love people. Most of the time I really, unironically do. At least most people. I think they're wonderful. Daffodils, puppies, and tacos delight me. There's enough beauty in the world to spend your whole life seeking it, and never have your fill.

I don't know what it's like to be other people, but on my good days, I love being me.

The walls of my soul are thin. Light streams in the cracks, and when I listen closely, I can hear the heartbeat of the world, pulsing away with a joy as poignant as grief. I am porous. It all slips through. In the excess of this technicolor universe where we live, I feel it all deeply.

I feel it *all* deeply.

MARIE.

I have sometimes privately wondered if I was more fragile than the average person.

Light soaks through my porous soul, but dark things slip through too. Sad and ugly things. I am the canary in the coal mine, singing my heart out because the walls are closing in. With my ear to the wall of the world, I hear a death rattle, lungs eaten up by loss, envy, hatred. The world I love so much—the birds and the sea and the sunshine—is polluted, not only with the haze of actual smog, but with the knowledge that someone, somewhere is suffering. I can't get it out of my head. I can't get it out of my heart. Sometimes when I see the news, I am seized, not with fear but sadness. When I look at all the senseless loss and cruelty, I can't imagine what we did to deserve this broken world. All is not as it should be. I'm not good at getting over things. They hang around me like the smell of a bonfire. I can't tell the difference between my calamity and the calamities of others. It's all sorrow, all smoke from the burning of my precious, beloved world.

I don't know what it's like to be other people, but on my bad days I can hardly bear it.

Joy Marie.

The same capacity that enables me to rejoice so fully makes me vulnerable to the great consuming pain and loss of our world. Some days holding these two worlds inside makes me feel like I have a superpower. I am like a carbon monoxide alarm for the world. Yes, the smallest of things can set me off—joyful or sorrowful—but isn't that the point of such a device? What good would an insensitive CO alarm be? But some days I just feel tired, fragile, like an overstimulated child. I worry that what I have mistaken for strength is only compacted grief.

> **The same capacity that enables me to rejoice so fully makes me vulnerable to the great consuming pain and loss of our world.**

My name announces it as true about me, but I think these wells of gladness and seas of sorrow live in all of us. We all contain multitudes. The frustrating thing is that it's nearly impossible to pick which emotions we experience. We can't really say, "I'll only have the happy ones, please. And sadness for Sundays. But never anger!" We can choose to cultivate an outlook on life that disposes us toward joy, yes. But if we actively try to suppress our stormy emotions, our ability to feel joy will also be stifled. You will exhaust yourself and cauterize your feelings. You won't have room to rejoice if you're in a constant game of whack-a-mole with your negative emotions.

So how do we live with these worlds inside us?

I love the Irish animated film *Song of the Sea*. The backstory is a retelling of the Celtic myth of a warrior king called Mac Lir ("son of the sea") and his mother, Macha, who is, inexplicably, an owl. Mac Lir suffered a broken heart and cried so much that he drowned the ocean. Hating to see her son suffer, Macha panicked and sought to stop his suffering in the only way she knew how, by turning him into stone. Head bent in grief, the giant became an island in the sea where the birds built their nests. The movie tells the story of two children who live on that island with a sorrow of their own: their mother disappeared. Their father's heart is broken, and like Macha in the story, their grandmother is concerned, insisting they move away from the island to live with her. After being taken to the city, the children escape and try to return to the island, encountering mythical figures, dancing fairies, and old-tale spinners as they go. But as the story wears on, the atmosphere becomes less merry. The magical creatures, even the good ones, begin to turn to stone.

The two stories become one; Mac Lir's sorrow is the sorrow of their father, and Macha's enchantments are the overbearing care of the grandmother. To keep the fairy from disappearing, they must speak to Macha and convince her to stop turning things into stone. After a perilous journey, they find her hidden in her magic nest, half-turned to stone herself. She is a real mess. She does not know what to do with emotion. It is terrifying to her. Each time she experiences an overpowering emotion—joy, anger, sadness—she bottles it up in a magic glass jar. Her house is strewn with little Mason jars filled with storm clouds and sunshine and red-hot fire. Stemming the tide of emotion has become an obsession. Remembering the grief of her beloved son, she would rather feel nothing than be vulnerable to the pain he endured. She makes herself into stone, impenetrable, invulnerable, safe. But if she bottles up all her sorrow, the world of fairies will turn to stone. And so will Macha.

She must undo the curse and let her heart become flesh again, must let Mac Lir cry his ocean. But what if his ocean of sadness drowns the world?

What if my boat of joy drowns in my sea of sorrow?

It's a fair question.

Getting Acquainted with Grief

The prophet Isaiah describes the servant of the Lord this way: "He is despised and rejected of men; a man of sorrows, and acquainted with grief" (Isaiah 53:3 KJV). I take great comfort in the idea that God chose to inhabit our fractured world, that Jesus willingly took on a body vulnerable to the common cold, stomach flus, and the violence of hateful people. I do not

34

know why our world is as broken as it is, or why God lets it be that way, but I know that God has not chosen indifference to our pain, but solidarity. God, who is above everything and all powerful, who did not need to be vulnerable, has bent low and become acquainted with sorrow. *Our* sorrow. *Your* sorrow. Thinking that, perhaps, I'm not alone in my sadness makes me a little braver.

But there's something else I love about this verse: the word *acquainted*. It makes grief sound like a person Jesus knew. Someone He talked with sometimes. It makes me think that if sorrow passed Jesus in the street, He would recognize it.

Are you acquainted with grief?

I think most of us have a relationship with grief more like that of Edward Rochester to Bertha Antoinetta Mason in *Jane Eyre*. (If you haven't read the book, this is a huge spoiler, but Bertha is the violent and unstable wife Rochester hides in his attic.) She's always there, but no one really knows about her, and for the most part life goes on as normal. Sometimes a particularly sensitive person will hear her rattling around upstairs, but if they ask about her, we change the subject, suspiciously deny their inquiries, or, if we're really in bad shape, demand that they leave our house immediately and go live with missionaries. But sometimes grief makes a fuss, banging around upstairs moaning and shrieking, maybe even lighting the curtains on fire. She's pitiful and we sort of resent her. She's keeping us from living a good life, marrying our sassy governess. We wish she would go away. But we feel a strange loyalty to her, like she needs care. If we leave her up there long enough, she'll eventually blind us and burn the whole house down.

Yes, for some of us grief is more like an unwanted houseguest than an acquaintance. She lives with us, but we don't speak to her.

There are so many reasons we may not feel able or willing to make the acquaintance of grief and her cousins, fear and anger. Perhaps in your family some emotions were only experienced as damaging: an angry father, a cripplingly depressed mother. Perhaps your brain, like mine, is wired with what we call mental illness. Perhaps in your world some emotions were simply verboten: anger, curiosity, sadness. Perhaps your religious community made you feel guilty for any "negative" emotions, as if you didn't have enough faith, as if you weren't a real Christian. Perhaps you have experienced deep trauma that has catastrophically unsettled your emotional universe. Perhaps you are simply afraid that if you started crying, you might never stop.

I have hidden from grief in my life too, or rather hidden her away, hoping she won't make a fuss. I'm never very successful. She finds her way into my life, sometimes in unexpected and often unpleasant ways. Anger I can't place. Fear I haven't dealt with. She pulls down a curtain, she lights a room on fire, she pushes someone I love away. Why am I so reticent to speak with her? I think it is because I'm afraid that grief will tell me the truth about the world, and that if I heard it, I could never really be happy again. I'm afraid sadness knows the secret heart of reality, and it is broken. I'm afraid that if I listened to her, grief would tell me that all there is in this life is loss, disappointment, betrayal, and then death. I'm afraid I would drown in the sea of sorrow.

But Jesus was acquainted with grief. And I wonder if I can be too.

So I resolve to make her acquaintance. When the world is quiet and no one is around, I take a deep breath and invite sadness to sit with me, to tell me her story. She begins by naming precious things: people I love, hopes I've cherished, imaginations of the way the world could have been, ways my life should have been if hurt and disappointment hadn't woven themselves into the fabric of my heart. She tells me these things have gone away. At first all I can hear is loss. All I can see is what I wished for, what I cherished, gone in a breath. I feel lost and desperately sad.

But as I call on all my strength to listen closely, I hear something I didn't expect.

Sadness tells me how precious the world is. She tells me how deeply she has loved, how dearly she has hoped, how fully she has trusted. She tells me that all those hopes meant something, pointed to the gladness beating at the heart of the world. She is indignant because she knows her birthright: wholeness, unity, growth. She weeps not because loss meant nothing, but because it meant a great, great deal. Her tears testify to the world we were meant for, that we should create for our children, that we taste in baptism. She has her ear to the wall of the world, and she knows it beats with beauty. She wrings her hands in sorrow that we have gotten so out of tune.

Sadness sings the same song that Joy sings.

In His most famous teaching, the Sermon on the Mount, Jesus says something remarkable: "Blessed are those who mourn, for they will be comforted" (Matthew 5:4). I've often puzzled over it. Aren't people who mourn the opposite of blessed? They've lost something. Their hearts are broken. But sadness has her wisdom too. Those who mourn do so because they cannot accept the brokenness of the world with equanimity. Their very indignation reflects a knowledge of the deeper reality of life: that it was meant to be good, whole, and full of joy, and that it is not. Those who mourn know the full value of what has been lost and refuse to forget it.

I've come to realize that sadness and happiness are sisters. They are both born of a tender heart that feels and responds to this world we love. Sadness tells the truth about the world: that there are things so precious and beautiful in this world that deserve to be mourned when they're lost.

Blessed are those who know it.

The King of the Jungle had it all wrong. He thought I could never feel sadness because I was joyful. But in my experience, the opposite is true. To rejoice, we must sometimes weep. The final scene of *The Song of the Sea* is just about perfect. Macha breaks her spell, and as she finally begins to experience all her pent-up emotions, the little glass jars explode, one by one. Sadness breaks as a rainstorm, tears spilling from her round owl eyes. Anger is a thunderstorm broiling with fury and cracking lightning strikes of rage. Happiness beams out as sunshine, an uncontrollable chirping of birds, and laughter. And as the emotions wash over Macha, the world begins to awaken. The dancing fairies frolic into life and play their fiddles. The storyteller shakes his long mane of hair, each strand full of stories. Mac Lir's dogs rise and run to find their master. Mac Lir awakens, scaring the birds that have come to nest on his long-bowed shoulders as he rises to stride onward to meet the sunrise. It is color and beauty and song and joy and grief all bound into one. A sea of sorrow, a deep well of joy. It's all very beautiful.

This is how I've come to imagine my thin-walled soul. Emotions are temporary things. They pass, if we let them. They are like waves on the sand; you can't do much to stop them, but they won't be there long. There's no use in being afraid of the weather.

This is what I want you to know: it is okay to be sad sometimes. It is okay to weep when your heart is broken. And if you've saved up sadness, you might have to weep for a long time. That's okay. I know what it's like. I'm sorry for the precious things you have lost, or never had. For the things that have broken your heart. For the things that have made you feel unsafe in the world. For the people who haven't been able to treat your wounds with the honor they deserve. If I could (and you didn't mind, of course) I would sit with you, and make you a cup of tea, and we would cry together over your sorrows. Because they deserve to be wept over.

And something else: we need other people to grieve with us, to teach us how to grieve well, how to sail through the sea of sorrow. We were not intended to sail alone. People say time heals all wounds, but I don't think that is true. Time can make some wounds fester and harden. Some wounds need a specialist to make sure they heal, whether that be a mentor, a spiritual director, a professional counselor, or a psychiatrist. Don't be afraid to ask. Sorrow doesn't make everyone kind. Tend to your sadness so that it becomes a source of deeper love and deeper joy, not deeper pain. Good sorrow heals. And, hear this: you are well worth the trouble. Your wounds are worth the effort. God wants wholeness for you.

Tend to your sadness so that it becomes a source of deeper love and deeper joy, not deeper pain.

I like how Tolkien puts it: "I will not say: do not weep; for not all tears are an evil."[1]

Do not be afraid to weep. But also, don't be afraid to laugh.

I want you to know something else: just because you may be sad now doesn't mean you won't someday be able to be incredibly, deeply, and uncomplicatedly happy. The funny thing about sadness is that it wants to convince us that it is the truest thing. And sadness is a true thing. But so is happiness. So are babies giggling, and daffodils in springtime, and salmon and lox bagels, and laughing so hard that your stomach hurts. Sadness is not somehow "more real." When your sadness has passed, let it be passed. The hardest thing is to let happiness and sadness both be true. But they are. So, when a storm has passed and you're feeling joyful and happy and thankful, ride the wave. Breathe deep relief and know that this too is true. It will feel frightening to rejoice, sometimes, because the vulnerability of joy is two breaths away from the vulnerability of sorrow.

When you throw your arms open in joy, sometimes you will get sucker-punched. But as far as I can tell, it's better to sail the sea of sorrow than to never let joy fill the sails of your boat.

To Read

A Grief Observed by C. S. Lewis

Notes on Grief by Chimamanda Ngozi Adichie

To See

The animated film *Song of the Sea* (2014) by Cartoon
  Saloon

To Listen

"Lacrimosa" by Wolfgang Amadeus Mozart

"So What" by Noah Gundersen

To Ponder

These artworks all deal with the theme of grief. *A Grief Observed* and *Notes on Grief* chronicle the universal and yet
particular experiences of grief from the perspectives of two
very different authors. *Song of the Sea* embodies grief and
sadness in fairy-tale form. Mozart's piece (meaning "weep-
ing/tearful") shows the grandeur of grief, and "So What" its
inevitability.

   Are you acquainted with grief? Make an appointment
with her today. What would make you feel safe enough to
experience both grief and joy? Who has taught you how to
sail the sea of sorrow?

2

Flounder well

Midway upon the journey of our life
I found myself within a forest dark,
For the straightforward pathway had been lost. . . .
But of the good . . . which there I found,
Speak will I. . . .

—Dante Alighieri, *Divine Comedy*

Dear Diary,

It is day 304 of the pandemic and we are, once again, in lock-down. I cannot remember if it is Tuesday, Friday, or February. All I know is that it is too cold for a walk, and I am extremely bored.

I have named the rook that lands on my roof Andrew. He is my only friend. Except my brother Joel, of course, but we don't speak anymore. Oh, no! We're not angry, but we've spent so much time in each other's company that there's simply nothing left to say. We have talked about literally everything.

43

People call on FaceTime and ask if anything new has happened. What an insensitive question! No! Absolutely nothing new has happened! The most exciting thing is that you can now order takeaway fish 'n chips on the Deliveroo app. Come to think of it, this is very exciting. I sigh sometimes when I think that I am in the prime of youth, full of vigor and beauty, locked in my tower with no one to admire me. I fret over what I will wear even with nowhere to go. I'm like the narrator of T. S. Eliot's "The Love Song of J. Alfred Prufrock":

> I grow old . . . I grow old . . .
> I shall wear the bottoms of my trousers rolled.
> Shall I part my hair behind? Do I dare to eat a peach?[1]

Speaking of parting my hair: if I paused to think about how long it has been since I got a haircut, I might be tempted to despair. So instead, I will simply say that my resemblance to a pre-Raphaelite muse grows more striking with each passing day. I suppose this adds a certain elegance to the misfortune of a wasted youth. I do live near a canal. Perhaps I could do a live reenactment of Tennyson's "The Lady of Shalott"? Only this would be very cold, for, as I have mentioned, it is winter, making it impossible to do almost anything outside.

Our only comfort is food and the BBC television series *All Creatures Great and Small*. Tonight we had steak because nothing means anything. Having no other earthly pleasures, we indulge in food. I suppose the main problem with all this is that we don't know how long it will last. Are we halfway through the woods? Or almost through them? Or is this like one of those video games with a glitch where you can walk through the same forest forever?

Anyway, must dash; *Murder, She Wrote* is on the television. I am full of ennui.

    Very best wishes,

    j

Finding Your Way Through Life's Dark Woods

As I write this book, we are smack-dab in the middle of a world in full flounder. The Covid-19 pandemic has raged on now for almost a year, straining health-care systems, devastating economies, snatching loved ones away from many families, and leaving the rest of us trapped in a seemingly eternal Groundhog Day of lockdown. When this started, it was all a bit cozy. Terrifying, yes, but also cozy. People were tucking into their nests, learning how to make sourdough bread, fantasizing about writing the next great novel, and celebrating the pollution-free skylines (nature is healing!). It was all very cute. It is no longer cute. We try to be optimists, but at the end of the day we have no idea when this will end, or if it will end.

We are, in short, floundering.

If there's one thing in life that I am good at, it is floundering. I am a grade-A flounderer. *Merriam-Webster* defines *flounder* in the following way: "to struggle to move or obtain footing: thrash about wildly."[2] I have spent a great deal of my life thrashing about wildly, not quite sure of where I was going, or what I was meant to be doing, or who I wanted to be. To thrash about for the purpose of "obtaining footing" implies that there exists some elusive state of stability that we simply haven't achieved yet. In my experience, the whole nature of floundering is that you're not quite sure what that state of sure footing is; you just know that you haven't reached it yet. So you thrash about wildly, hoping to God that you are thrashing in the right direction, painfully aware that all your energy may be for naught. Which ties in nicely with the secondary definition of flounder: "to proceed or act clumsily or ineffectually."[3] Sound familiar? Or am I the only one?

It makes me think of the opening lines to Dante Alighieri's *Divine Comedy*, which I quoted at the opening of this chapter.

Many of us wake up at some point in our journey of life to discover that "the straightforward pathway had been lost." We feel like we are in a bad dream. We can't figure out which direction is up, or if we're moving forward or backward. These seasons can feel like a waste, like if we could only make it out of the dark wood, if we could only stop floundering, we could begin living. I have some bad and good news: most of life is in this dark wood. We think we will obtain sure footing after a certain milestone is passed, or an obstacle is mastered. *Things will be different, sturdier, make more sense, we tell ourselves, when I have finished college . . . when I get a job . . . when I get married . . . when I have a baby . . . when the baby is out of diapers . . .* The list goes on and on, as we wait to feel like we have arrived, or even just know in which direction we are headed. The nature of this life is that we never "arrive." Saint Augustine describes the Christian life as a pilgrimage, straining for a destination we cannot reach in life. In doing this, he draws from Hebrews 11: "All these people were still living by faith when they died. They did not receive the things promised; they only saw them and welcomed them from a distance, admitting that they were foreigners and strangers on earth" (v. 13).

This is life.

We often don't know where we're going, or how things will turn out. There is not a magic wand that can bop us on the head and reveal exactly what we should be doing, or whom we should marry, or how to move forward. And even when the events we hoped for happen, we sometimes still feel confused. For better or worse, most of life is in the in-between. But there's good news too: treasures can be found in the floundering. Dante says that's what he'll write about. My favorite translation puts it this way: "My theme will be the good I found there."[4] In my life, I have found that though I felt lost, those floundering seasons were often forming, deepening, and directing me in profound ways I couldn't see. With the wisdom of hindsight, I would tell my former, floundering self to lean in to this season, to be faithful to it, to trust that seeds are growing even though you can't see them, to use the empty time well. I've learned that there are better and worse ways to flounder; it takes practice to flounder well. In this chapter, I'll share my tips for effectual floundering.

Though I felt lost, those floundering seasons were often forming, deepening, and directing me in profound ways I couldn't see.

Listen to Your Life

I once heard a Navy SEAL say that people tend to drown because they waste all their energy trying not to drown. A person drowning is more likely to survive if they simply relax, take deep intentional breaths, and float. This is the opposite of what our bodies tell us to do. As soon as we perceive ourselves to be in danger, a rush of adrenaline hits, we panic, and our bodies scream "FIGHT! FLY! FLOUNDER!" We waste precious energy grasping for something only relaxation, lack of movement, and trust can achieve. The great irony is that our survival instincts can actually be quite perilous, tricking us into untimely death.

I've found the same to be true in life. When we feel lost in the dark wood, our first impulse is to panic, to swim, to move, afraid we'll get stuck in the forest at night (or stuck at a bad job! or never get married! or fade into the amorphous meaninglessness of early parenthood! forever!). We flounder, thrashing about wildly because we're afraid we'll get stuck or sink, ironically making ourselves all the more likely to succumb to the waves of life out of pure exhaustion. Movement is a senseless waste of energy if you don't know where you're going, and if something is tied to your ankle, no matter how fast you run, it will chase you.

The first key to floundering well is to stop moving, accept your life, and listen.

It all boils down to comedic improv.

I was a theater kid in high school, and while I now squirm at the thought of performing improv for an audience, when I was young, I really enjoyed it. There are many different improv games, usually involving some element of impromptu and humorous storytelling, but there is one rule that is the foundation of all of them: "yes, and."

YES. You cannot reject any part of the reality that your fellow actor presents to you in the scene you act out. If they say, "The purple elephant has gotten out of the grocery store," you must proceed with appropriate urgency to consider how one might contain and subdue a rampaging purple elephant. You must accept, fully and creatively, the reality you are presented. AND. As long as you have accepted the reality of your scene partner, you may add anything to the story you like. With your "and" you can add an elephant hypnotist, a snowstorm, or Gandalf the Grey. Your partner must also listen. They too must "yes, and." The scene comes to life as a result of your mutual and generative acceptance of whatever imagination throws your way.

It is easy to think that success at improv comes from being a wild storyteller, or a shameless ham, but the best improvisers are good listeners. People who are unable to listen, unable to say "yes," are often a bit awkward, overpowering. They may say some funny things, but they preclude the real joy of improv: the reciprocity between the actors, the give-and-take of co-creating a funny scene. It's hard work, but nothing is as gratifying as the soaring satisfaction of making a whole room of people howl with uncontrollable laughter.

Life is like improv, and those who seek to flounder well should take note of its rules.

YES. We may not like the scene (or life) in which we find ourselves, but we have to accept it for what it is. That's just the game! We all find ourselves in stories that are not entirely of our own making. If we ruled the world, there are aspects of our stories we would not have included: personal flaws, setbacks, difficult family members, emotional wounds, financial problems, romantic disappointments. But there they are, rampaging through our lives like feral purple elephants. Watching people who are not good at accepting the reality of their scene partners is a painful experience; so is watching someone who does not acknowledge the reality of their life. Accepting life, with all its warts and wounds included, does not mean surrender, or even approval of its brokenness; it simply means grappling with life as it is, with no illusions.

AND. Once we have accepted our lives as they are, regrets and radiances alike, we can begin to shape our stories. Only when we see life with clear eyes and stubborn acceptance can we add our "and" to life. We can make something of this story, this life, with all its limitations and setbacks, weird characters, and unspectacular settings. A good improviser can make any scene exciting.

Trying to "and" your life before you have said "yes" to it is the recipe for ineffectual floundering. But it's more difficult to say yes to life than you might think.

We humans are masters of self-deception, always convincing ourselves that we're in a different story than we actually are, trying to make people into villains or heroes when they're only humans, convincing ourselves that we're beyond repair or reproach. Sometimes we avoid saying yes to life because we are afraid of looking life square in the eye, afraid we'll find unspent griefs, unmet desires, regret, and shame. We would rather wrestle with an illusion than be disappointed by reality. So we thrash about, proceeding clumsily and ineffectually. We waste energy, wishing or pretending our life is other than it is.

> Once we have accepted our lives as they are, regrets and radiances alike, we can begin to shape our stories.

And as we thrash, we lose energy. We begin to sink, sink, sink.

There is a poem I recite to myself when I'm struggling to say yes to my life. It is by the English poet and priest Malcolm

Guite. Each line is like a precious trinket I keep in a little box and pull out from time to time when I need it. It goes like this:

> Begin the song exactly where you are.
> Remain within the world of which you're made.
> Call nothing common in the earth or air.
>
> Accept it all and let it be for good.
> Start with the very breath you breathe in now,
> This moment's pulse, this rhythm in your blood
>
> And listen to it, ringing soft and low.
> Stay with the music, words will come in time.
> Slow down your breathing. Keep it deep and slow.
>
> Become an open singing bowl, whose chime
> Is richness rising out of emptiness,
> And timelessness resounding into time.
>
> And when the heart is full of quietness
> Begin the song exactly where you are.[5]

This poem is about a singing bowl, an instrument that seems to have been developed in the eleventh century BCE in China and used as a tool for meditation, music making, and relaxation. It's a small metal bowl around which you run a wooden dowel. At first, nothing seems to be happening, and then, as the wooden mallet creates almost indiscernible vibrations, the bowl begins to sing. The person playing the singing bowl must be patient, because if their movement is not slow and smooth, the dowel will bounce and disturb the development of the slow vibrations that create the song of the bowl. Some bowls have a low resonant bass tone like the sustained belching of a bullfrog; some have a crystal-high voice like a stream tumbling over pebbles. Each song is beautifully different, just like our own lives and stories. Guite uses the singing bowl as a metaphor for prayer. We go to God, wanting answers, direction, a sense of inner resonance. But so often, our very disposition stands in the way of the outcome we desire. We rush the dowel around the bowl, demanding it sing when our racket and movement are preventing the very song we desire. We blame God for His silence when all we've been doing is shouting. We must stop floundering. "Be still, and know that I am God," writes the psalmist (46:10). We must be patient, slow, steady. We must accept this moment, not try to rush to the next one.

We must learn to sing.

When you are floundering, begin the song exactly where you are. Try not to predict the future or litigate the past. Do not wish you were someone else. Accept the fullness and emptiness of your life. God's voice is quiet. Listen to the soft, low hum of your life. There is a song there, and only in quietness will you learn to sing it. Say yes to your life. The song will come in time.

Become the Most Interesting (Wo)man in the World

> At museums he's allowed to touch the art.
> He once parallel parked a train.
> On every continent in the world, there is a sandwich
>   named after him.
> His hands feel like rich brown suede.
> He can speak French . . . in Russian.
> His shirts never wrinkle.

He once had an awkward moment, just to see how it
feels.

Once while sailing around the world, he discovered a
shortcut.

In a past life, he was himself.

He's . . . the most interesting man in the world.

These are just a few of the best lines from the successful ad
campaign for Dos Equis beer, featuring the most interesting
man in the world himself: Jonathan Goldsmith, a tuxedoed
gentleman whose leathered skin and perfectly groomed beard
ooze adventure, intelligence, and sophistication. Each commer-
cial features vintage footage of an adventurous life (sword-
fighting a samurai, riding a jet-black horse through a ballroom)
and concludes with Goldsmith raising a glass of beer and saying, "I don't always drink beer, but when I do, it's Dos Equis."
The brand manages to promise its consumers that by choosing
Dos Equis, they will not only enjoy a good alcoholic beverage,
but lead a leisured and interesting life as well. *You will be more
interesting if you drink this beer* it seems to promise. More
cultured. More complex. More of a man.

Why is this ad so effective? I think it is because it reminds
us of the potential that lies dormant in human nature, all that
we could be, the aspects of our humanity we could access, but
usually don't.

Every human being has the potential to be endlessly interesting. And that includes you. We assume that some people
are just born cool and emerge from the womb interesting.
But I don't think this is true. Sure, some people have naturally flashy personalities, but we are all capable of wild and

wonderful things. Within us all are innumerable skills *in potentia*. We can salsa dance. We can spin words into poetry and stories. We can make amazing things: from bread to Bolognese to Sacher tortes to guacamole. We can be so regal that you want to bow down, so silly that you burst out in laughter, so heartrending that you could weep forever. We can fight for justice, give generously, tell jokes. We can make clothes and design fashions and create hairstyles. There is this guy who carves designs with a rake into the sand on the beaches near my house. Whenever I pass on the hill above and see a quarter of a mile of swirling patterns that the tide will soon wash away, I think to myself, *Human beings are so weird, so full of potential. They can do the coolest stuff.* But they often don't. They are often quite boring.

Why are we often so boring?

I think our world has the tendency to turn us into one-dimensional people, valuing only one aspect of our humanity to the detriment of all the others. Often, that monomania tends to be "work" and "productivity," though tedium can march under other banners too ("piety" and "responsibility," even "sociability"). These values are so central that we have a hard time evaluating our lives by any other measure. We panic when we don't have a clear sense of our *purpose*, our *usefulness*, of what we're *accomplishing*, whether it is in school, our job, or our church. Thus, even though there's a lot more to us than "accomplishment," we put all our effort into one aspect of our lives, and the other parts of us remain underdeveloped. We become like a guy at the gym who always misses leg day; some aspects of our personhood are strong and taut, while other parts of ourselves are atrophied and scrawny. Our "accomplishment" muscles are strong, but our relational, adventurous, intellectual, romantic, and creative muscles dwindle. We have an overemphasis on "doing" and an underemphasis on "becoming."

This is often brought to the forefront by seasons of floundering. I've noticed that my floundering seasons often coincide with a loss of feeling purposeful or useful. I floundered when I finished my undergraduate degree, suddenly discovering there was no clear-cut path of what to do next, no grades to tell me I was doing a good job, no semester handbook to tell me what I should do next. Friends have reported a similar feeling when they first had kids; here is an endless task with no markers of success or usefulness. How can I know who I am?

The great thing about floundering is that it usually creates empty space in your life, which presents the opportunity to exercise other muscles, the room to try on different parts of yourself, the time to explore different ideas, skills, experiences. I mean, look at you! You're reading this book, which indicates some space in your life. The yawning chasm of free time after college (even though I had three jobs) terrified me. That empty space, however, proved to be an opportunity for me to become a more interesting person. I read more than I had ever read that year, I discovered new musicians I loved, I traveled when finances allowed, I learned to bake.

In short, I became a more interesting person.

So here's my challenge: if you are floundering, make it your goal to become the Most Interesting Person in the World. This is the opposite side of the coin from listening to your life. I've already said you should reject the urge to fill every empty moment with meaningless movement toward an imagined "somewhere."

But emptiness also begs to be filled—so fill it well! Don't fill in the crevices of your life with work but with interest. Become an interesting person. You might as well. What else do you have to do?

Here's what I mean: do the thing you've always thought would be cool, but you didn't have time to do. The summer before I began my PhD coursework, I resolved to read a book on physics. This was something I was interested in learning more about, and I figured I wouldn't have time to read it during my doctorate. I took it with me everywhere, reading a few pages on my parents' back porch, in the morning while camping with a friend in the mountains, on the airplane back to Scotland. To be honest, I probably only comprehended about 30 percent of the book's content, the rest of it simply flying unimpeded over my sweet little arts-and-humanities head. But the 30 percent that I got, I really got. I've heard it said that a little science turns you into an atheist, and a lot of science turns you back into a believer. This entirely secular book left me with an attitude of awe at this universe we call home, and at least a foggy idea of what a photon is. (Have you ever heard of quantum entanglement? It is so cool! Put down this book! Google it immediately!)

Reading a book on physics did not immediately contribute to any of my career plans, but it made me a more knowledgeable human being, more fully developed to interact with the world, and more amazed at the intricacy and grandeur of the universe. It used a muscle that had been out of practice. Becoming an interesting person is about learning to use all the muscles of your humanity. Scripture says to "love the Lord your God with all your heart and with all your soul and with all your mind and with all your strength" (Mark 12:30). It is easy to spiritualize this verse, as though we only love God with our minds by thinking about God. But I like to think that living into the fullness of our capacities in each of these areas *is* loving God. It is not merely about the content of our loving, but the preposition; we do these things *with* God. When we use our minds to ponder the complexities of quantum entanglement, we are loving God with our minds. When we run a marathon, or reach the top of our class, or salsa dance, we are loving God with our strength. When we love someone with our whole heart or pour all that we are into a cause that matters, we are loving God with our soul. Let's not give God less credit than God deserves. If God created us with the capacity to be interesting, skilled, intelligent, and cultured, why do we assume God only desires placid little devotees who read only Bible study books and eat only oatmeal?

Becoming an interesting person is an opportunity to show off how cool God made humans to be. And I am doing my best to be extremely cool.

In your efforts to flounder well, think strategically through different areas of your humanity in which you'd like to grow. Here are a few ideas:

Think about how you might want to develop emotionally and socially. Are there issues from your past or family you haven't dealt with? Perhaps now is the time to become a more emotionally mature person (there's nothing more interesting than an emotionally mature person!). You could seek a counselor or make a list of books or podcasts that might help you grow. Are you a good friend? Make it a point to invest in friendships and a social life. Host a soiree at your house!

Consider both your knowledge and your intellectual abilities. Make a list of books you've always wanted to read and start working your way through. (P.S. Audiobooks help!). Pick a topic you want to be an expert in and find every podcast, video, and book you can on that topic. Try learning or brushing up on a language—download a language learning app, watch a foreign language film. If you feel overwhelmed, remember: the mind is a muscle you stretch. The more you try, the easier it will get. You can't always see how much stronger you're already getting.

Think about how you nurture and grow your faith and spiritual life. Have you "spiritually self-actualized" or are you just adopting the stale faith (or non-faith) of your family or culture of origin? Have you explored this dimension of your humanity? What would it look like for you to go deeper? To shake off some of the old habits or wrong beliefs you inherited? Have you ever thought about trying a different church or seeing a spiritual director? What questions bug you? What books could you read to explore your questions? What makes your soul feel alive?

Think about both your physical prowess and your practical skills in life. What is one skill you wish you had? Changing a tire? Woodcarving? Look up YouTube videos, local classes, clubs. Learn to cook. There's nothing more rewarding. Have you always wanted to dance? Join a local studio or look up dance tutorials online. Do you have a personal style? Think about it, and put a little more time into the physical, visible self you present to the world. Pro tip: try lipstick.

These are just a few ideas. I'm sure you have others. Because you are an interesting person.

Don't Be a Total Mess

Once, in one of my ritual rounds of bellyaching about who, what, where, or how I wanted to be in the world, my mother gave me the following advice: "Joy, don't wait to be a grown-up until you get married. Buy the nice sheets. Save for a house. Make a home. Have traditions. You may never get married! So why wait?" Being in a state of angst, I of course immediately responded with indignation for my mother's pessimism regarding my romantic future ("Thanks for the vote of confidence, Mom!"), but the advice was good and, in light of floundering, I would like to pass it on to you: while you flounder, live well. And more particularly: make a home and glory in it.

For a variety of reasons, my generation is notorious for not being able to reach milestones of adulthood that used to be inevitable. Before you blame it all on avocado toast and arrested development, consider our plight. The cost of living has skyrocketed while the average income has stabilized. The job market has increasingly higher hurdles of entry, leading many of my peers to attend college and incur huge amounts of debt because they thought it was what you did to get a job, only to be greeted by the "gig economy," where we get along by patching together a hodgepodge of employment. It's no wonder that so many of us live with family. And if living with your family doesn't kill the romantic mood, then economic despair does, which at least partially explains the historically low levels of marriage, coupling, and childbearing.

> **While you flounder, live well. Make a home and glory in it.**

Perhaps you're reading this and thinking it doesn't describe you. If you've managed to transcend the employment rat race or the dating (cess)pool, God bless you! Enjoy your life, unicorn! I'm sure you have unique troubles of your own.

But for the rest of us, it presents a challenge. As someone more serious than me once wrote: how now shall we live?[6] How do we make good lives waiting for things we may never attain? Enter Sally-mama advice: don't wait to be a grown-up.

Being an adult is not about how much money is in your bank account, your relational status, or your career prospects. An adult is someone who is in charge of their life and who regards themself with the respect befitting that role. I think many people spend most of their adult lives without regarding themselves this way, which has a psychological effect. You take neither as much responsibility nor as much pleasure in ordering your life as you should. But nothing helps cure floundering as much as taking responsibility for and pleasure in the rhythms of your life.

I think this involves two things. First: *don't be a total mess.*

I read a blog/poem by Sufjan Stevens that expressed this desire: "I don't want to be a total mess."[7] I think that this is a highly underrated aspiration. I like it because it's not too audacious; you can still be a *mess*, just not a *total mess.* But it also points to the fact that we should, on some level, be attempting to order our lives. I have great news for you: as an adult, you have the capacity to bring some order and dignity to your life. Many of us still live our lives like college freshmen: we stay up to all hours of the night, and we have a mismatched assortment of dishes and an inadequate supply of silverware. We sleep on the old, sad pillows that we've had forever and sigh when we observe our mismatched pj's in the mirror. We have not given ourselves either the permission or the impetus to really tame our lives.

But you can tame your life! You can bring order out of chaos! And it will feel good when you do!

The word *cosmetics* finds its origins in the Greek word *kosmos*, which means "order." This word is used in the Greek rendering of Genesis 1:1: "In the beginning God created the heavens and the earth." This act of creation is described as an ordering and filling of what was previously chaotic and empty ("The earth was formless and empty," v. 2). Words like *cosmopolitan* and *cosmetics* hold similar associations, referencing actions that bring order, harmony, and beauty to an otherwise chaotic reality. As people made in the image of God, we have the capacity to bring cosmos out of chaos. And I have found that bringing even a small amount of order and beauty to your floundering, messy life can have a great effect. For me, one way of practicing this is by how I dress. During the endless mush that was life in lockdown, I made it a point to dress well every day. Though the world may fall to pieces, I will be wearing something cute, my hair will be clean, and I will be sporting a brave shade of lipstick.

This small act of defiance made me feel less out of control and reminded me of how much power I have to bring life and beauty to my world. It also reminded me that my self-respect is not dependent on the circumstances of my life. I will not wait for the perfect circumstances to bring order to my life. There are little ways you can bring cosmos to your chaos. At some point in my life, I banned myself from working while I ate. I made it a point to sit down for five minutes, not look at my phone, and eat like a dignified human being. Even if it was only vases I purchased from a charity shop, or an artistic collage of postcards, I started to decorate my house like it wasn't a dorm room. I started going to sleep earlier. I acquired houseplants. The best-kept secret is that living like an adult is actually very fun. You get to determine how you will dress, what kind of food you like, how late you will stay up on weekends. Being an adult doesn't mean fitting into some predetermined box of how adults should live; it means relishing your role as queen (or king) of your life, creating a life of order and simplicity, which becomes a source of stability to others. And that reminds me of the other thing.

Treat yourself.

If you are the king or queen of your life, you also deserve some delight. I think there is a symbolic item in all of our minds that we put off buying until some mysterious future point when we will be stable adults. For one of my friends, it is a set of nice knives. He is now in his thirties and is a very competent cook, but he is often impeded by his subpar kitchen knives. I once asked him why he didn't buy new ones. He furrowed his eyebrows and cocked his head. "I don't know. I suppose I'm just waiting till I feel more permanent." He has a stable full-time job at a good university and lives in a flat he owns . . . if he's not stable, there's no hope for the rest of us!

What is that item for you? A new set of sheets? Real shoes? I want you to do something: treat yourself to the little luxury that you have holed away in your mind as the thing you will get or do as an adult. Being an adult is not only about the duties of organizing your life; it is about regarding yourself as a person who matters. We may take on the duties of adulthood without ever allowing ourselves the delight. We await some imagined moment when we will have finally arrived. Regard yourself with the respect that the responsibility you take for your life merits.

Often, finances stand in the way of conducting our lives in a way befitting our adulthood. But in my own life, I have also found that I sometimes make my life more bare bones than I need do. I keep myself from simple pleasures, from the hypothetical knife set, because it is a thing I will do someday when I have really arrived. In reality, some of the things I would do in that imagined future are not so out of reach financially as I make them out to be. There are simple, inexpensive ways to treat yourself like an adult. Perhaps it is something as simple as allowing yourself the luxury of buying flowers or a beautifully scented candle every month. As much as I can, I try to get out of my way and indulge in small luxuries that remind me that I am not an eternally desperate college freshman—I am queen of my domain. And tending to that domain becomes a blessing to all who enter it. If you're going to flounder, you may as well do it in a beautifully decorated apartment, wearing lipstick, and eating real meals.

So try not to be a total mess.

It's actually great fun.

Dear Diary,

As I write this, spring is beginning to loosen the vise grip of winter. Andrew the crow still sits desultorily on the roof, but bright-pink blossoms are opening optimistically around him, promising warmth and beauty and summertime. They make me catch my breath; I almost believe them.

To tell the truth, I now have a different dark wood ahead of me.

The spring is come, and with it hope, but one chapter of my life is closing, and I don't know what the next one will be. The old familiar lurch in my stomach alerts me to the fact that I might be wandering once again into the dark wood. But oddly, I don't mind. It feels almost familiar. I've been here before. I know what to do.

Listen to my life.

Become the most interesting woman in the world.

Don't be a total mess.

And at least I can get a takeaway coffee now.

Peace,

j

To Read

"Singing Bowl" by Malcolm Guite

Miss Rumphius by Barbara Cooney

To See

Sabrina (1995) starring Harrison Ford and Julia Ormond

To Listen

"Witness Trees" by Henry Jamison

Anything improvised by artists like John Coltrane and Miles
  Davis

To Ponder

These artworks focus on two sides of the coin of floundering well: accepting your life as it is, and making something
beautiful of it. Yes, And.

How did they flounder well? Malcolm Guite's poem and
Henry Jamison's song both focus on reconciling oneself to
seasons of disorder, confusion, and disarray. *Miss Rumphius*
and *Sabrina* are both about women who are disappointed
by life and yet derive great elegance, joy, and direction out
of floundering seasons. John Coltrane is a living embodiment of the great joyful art of improvisation.

Are you floundering now? How might you flounder
better? What have your floundering seasons in the past
taught you?

3

Remember: you have a body!

Pain and sorrow are assuaged by sleep and baths.

—Saint Thomas Aquinas, *Summa Theologica*

I once went on an unforgettable trip to Paris. It was the spring of my first year of grad school. After months of plotting and scheming, three of my best friends and I escaped the chilly gloom of Scotland for the rose-colored romance of France in February. Macie had lived with family just outside of Paris for a year, so she was our guide and translator. We planned and dreamed and packed our prettiest clothes (it was Paris, after all!) and counted down the days, ready for the trip of a lifetime. It was unforgettable for mostly good reasons.

Oh! What a trip it was. We ordered fresh croissants and crepes and cappuccinos from hole-in-the-wall cafes. We wandered along the Seine at night and basked in the golden glow of lights reflecting in the water. We saw the Eiffel Tower peeking out from a secret street full of locals sprawled outside cafes, lazily sipping wine. We ate an indecent amount of cheese paired with unbelievably cheap (and delicious!) wine and wore lipstick every day. We had adventures just dangerous enough to make for good stories, but not enough to really scare us. We marveled at the Sacré-Coeur and relished every multicolored corner of Montmartre and laughed at street performers. We were as happy and carefree and whimsical as a Joni Mitchell song. And we all got along famously.

That is, until the final day.

It all started because we had been in too much of a hurry getting all our things packed to have breakfast. Weighed down with our backpacks, we hopped on the metro with a few final sights to see. We stopped at an art gallery first, and then Macie wanted to take a picture in front of the Eiffel Tower for her French grandmother. It was a bit out of our way, but considering that the Eiffel Tower is sort of a Thing to Do, we resolved to take the metro there, then to Notre Dame and Shakespeare and Company, before getting a cab to the airport. At first, the adrenaline kept us all going, but by noon, we were fading. Well, *I* was fading.

By the time we found ourselves traversing the dusty, pebbled path leading away from the front of the Eiffel Tower, my blood sugar was in free fall. I felt hollow and a little bit shaky, but most of all I seethed with irritation. At the time, I had not put my finger on the fact that I was hungry, and so my "hanger" cast about wrathfully for an object or explanation. I settled on being annoyed that we were going to the Eiffel Tower for a second time. We had already *been* to the Eiffel Tower. *Why did we have to go again?* I thought as I passed a glorious flowering tree. *Nobody cares what I want,* I privately grumbled as we passed a perfectly charming string quartet. I did not vocalize any of this, but I must have exuded prickles because Rebecca, the tall, quiet redhead of the group, eyed me suspiciously from behind her sunglasses.

The Eiffel Tower, if you have not gathered this, is very tall, and so to get a passable picture you have to walk a few minutes along the path in front of it. So, after five minutes of strolling, we finally paused to take a few pictures. We took some together (in which I look surprisingly happy!), and finally Macie went to take a picture for her grandmother. She took some, and then there was a momentary setback: wrong setting on the camera. She went to pose again.

It was at this point that my hanger finally took over. Allegedly, I crossed my arms and saltily demanded, "Just how long are we going to be doing this?"

I must pause and remind you that in this moment, the moment in which I rudely demanded that my friend who was taking a *sentimental picture* for her French grandmother (!) do so more quickly, I was with three of my best friends in PARIS, on a beautiful spring day, standing in front of the EIFFEL TOWER, with the smell of Nutella crepes tickling my nostrils, blossoming trees framing a blue sky, and a string quartet playing Vivaldi in the background. And I was SULLEN.

I think Jenna laughed, Rebecca eyed me like a dangerous explosive object, and Macie responded with something along the lines of "I'm sorry! Is the Eiffel Tower too boring for you?"

This story ends happily, because I have good friends. Jenna appraised the situation, quickly deduced that this was a case of hypoglycemia-induced hanger, and ferried my surly self to the closest cafe. It was a cafe where instead of paying for food, you paid an hourly rate for a table and could eat whatever you wanted from the self-serve stations. I gloomily perused a shelf of vegetables and plopped down to dutifully eat while the others chatted cheerfully away. Fed wholesomely upon carrots, hummus, toast, and cheese, I slowly began to feel less morose, and in the place of my grumpiness, a sense of shame over my behavior began to grow. I hadn't said anything for twenty minutes or so, and as my faculties began to sharpen, and as I tuned in to the conversation, I discovered they were talking about one of my favorite topics: breakfast.

I think I misheard her, but Macie said something that sounded like "breakfast party," which caused my mind to explode with excitement over the prospect of two things I loved: breakfast and parties.

"BREAKFAST PARTY?" I almost shouted, to my own great surprise.

All three of my friends swiveled to look at me.

"Feeling better?" Jenna laughed. I confessed that I was and apologized for being such an angry lump. They were all gracious and forgiving, and we had a lovely conclusion to our Paris trip. Jenna hosted a Breakfast Party for my birthday that year, where I received my due penance for my hangry episode through a vivid retelling of the incident by Macie.

I've never lived it down.

I wish I could say this was the only time hunger has almost made me go nuclear, but I blush when I think of how many heated arguments, existential crises, and panic attacks I have had, only to realize that it is simply because I had skipped a meal. I'm told that in some recovery programs, they teach you an acronym aimed to interrupt a tailspin. You're taught to HALT! Check in with yourself to see if you are Hungry, Angry, Lonely, or Tired. And in about eighty percent of my minor crises, the first letter is to blame: I am hungry.

The ability to discern the difference between a valid existential crisis and a case of low blood sugar is a highly valuable skill, and yet mysteriously difficult to master. There is a story in the book of 1 Kings that I love. It is about the prophet Elijah, who is objectively one of the coolest people in the Bible. He raised people from the dead, called down fire from heaven, and when all was said and done, didn't die, but instead ascended into heaven on a flaming chariot. His name means "The Lord is my God," but he was sometimes called the "troubler of Israel" (1 Kings 18:17) because of his relentlessness in rejecting false gods. What a man!

The story takes place shortly after Elijah has had his most impressive standoff with the priests of Baal (1 Kings 18). He mercilessly mocks the priests who moan and wail and cut themselves in an effort to get Baal (their god) to call down fire on their altar, thus proving his superiority to the God of Israel. "Perhaps he is deep in thought, or busy, or traveling. Maybe he is sleeping and must be awakened," (1 Kings 18:27) chides Elijah, who seems to be enjoying witnessing all their fruitless endeavors too much. Being something of a showman, Elijah douses his altar with water three times (just to prove the point) and calls upon God to show His power. God engulfs the whole thing in fire from heaven. It is a decisive victory for Elijah, the great man of God.

But only one chapter later, we find Elijah sitting under a broom bush wishing that he could die.

"'I have had enough, LORD,' he said. 'Take my life'" (1 Kings 19:4).

I should mention that after the showdown, the bloodthirsty Queen Jezebel found out about the whole situation and sent word to Elijah that she intended to kill him the next day. This does dampen things slightly, but it's not as though this hasn't happened before. It is Jezebel's modus operandi to swear revenge upon her enemies. And anyway, had God not just engulfed a whole valley in flames to prove that Baal is not powerful? But when you're tired and your enemies have tied your laces as you try to run away, it's hard to see victory.

So Elijah has his little outburst and then he falls asleep.

What will God do here? Will God rebuke Elijah for his lack of faith? Show him a heavenly vision or a breathtaking miracle? Perhaps God will send a message of judgment or encouragement?

But no. This is what happens:

An angel touches Elijah, and he wakes up.

A platter of piping hot bread and a jar of cool, clean water await him.

"Get up and eat," says the angel.

So he does. And then he falls asleep again. A second time the angel comes to Elijah.

"Get up and eat, for the journey is too much for you" (1 Kings 19:5–7).

No heavenly vision. No prophetic word. Just instructions to eat and nap. So Elijah does. The next day, Elijah makes his way across the desert to a cliffside. God asks him what he's doing there.

He replied, "I have been very zealous for the LORD God Almighty. The Israelites have rejected your covenant, torn down your altars, and put your prophets to death with the sword. I am the only one left, and now they are trying to kill me too."

1 Kings 19:10

Elijah was in a full tailspin. He was Hungry, Angry, Lonely, and Tired. God's response always cuts me to the heart: God is not harsh with Elijah, and not even "spiritual." God does not rebuke Elijah for not having enough faith. God treats him a bit like a grumpy toddler: God touches him, gives him food and water, causes him to sleep. And once Elijah is stable enough to listen, God reminds him that he is not alone.

Somehow, it comforts me to know that even Elijah, the "troubler of Israel" and mighty prophet of God, fell victim to hunger-induced despair. And it comforts me all the more to know that God dealt with Elijah's outburst in pretty much the same way Jenna dealt with mine: amused compassion, naps, and a snack. Never underestimate the spiritual power of a nap and a snack.

Accidental Gnostics

It was my mother who first told me Elijah's story, and she told it with a wry smile because she knows me. It drives me crazy that all my loved ones know this weakness in me, but there's no getting around it: I'm a little fragile. I'm hypoglycemic. I have extremely low blood pressure. I have migraines and asthma and have been known to dramatically black out at inconvenient moments. My physical frailty doesn't match my self-perception. I imagine myself as a mighty woman, her sleeves rolled up, with endless grit, energy, and self-control. The reality is much

73

different. Part of the problem is that I'm too heavenly minded for my earthly good. I forget to take care of myself and then am shocked when my body rebels on me. I don't wish my body any ill; it just seems extremely inconvenient that I have to eat, sleep, and drink every day. How relentless! How inefficient! Why can't we just eat once a week? Sleep once a month?

I am in a constant battle to remember that I have a body and not to despise its limitations.

Somehow, I find it comforting that this is a battle as old as the church itself. Much older, in fact. One of the earliest and most persistent heresies was some form of gnosticism. Gnosticism comes from the Greek word *gnōsis*, meaning "knowledge" or "illumination." Gnostics believed that the material world is the source of evil from which humankind needs to be saved, and that to accomplish this salvation, we need to achieve a state of spiritual enlightenment. To gnostics, bodies are signs of our entrapment; we can only be free and whole if we escape these earthly flesh vessels that are always doing embarrassing things like eating, sleeping, crying, drinking, and making love. When tangled up with Christianity, gnosticism interpreted Jesus' life and ministry as a means of escaping the body for the sake of living a more "spiritual" and therefore "real" life.

I often live like a gnostic. I act as though being a Christian is about some kind of secret spiritual knowledge that is separate from (and better than!) the relentless demands of my selfish flesh vessel. I think many of us act this way, subconsciously seeing our bodies as impediments, inconveniences to the "more important" work of fulfilling our purpose, serving people, being spiritual (whatever that means!). When we break down, feel exhausted, cry, or have a panic attack, we regard it as weakness or immaturity. We have forgotten that we have bodies.

This was most obvious to me when I worked as a resident assistant at my undergraduate university. Prior to commencing our year of corralling unruly freshmen, we were sent on a retreat, given a quiet place with a journal and a notebook in which the following prayer (paraphrased) was written:

> *I am not God.*
> *I have a body.*
> *I am limited.*
> *I cannot be everywhere at once.*
> *I cannot fulfill everyone's needs.*
> *If I do not eat, I will starve.*
> *If I do not sleep, I will die.*
> *I am a creature of God, and just like His other creatures,*
> *I must eat,*
> *I must sleep,*
> *I must drink,*
> *I must have shelter,*
> *I must be comforted by those I love.*
> *I am limited.*
> *I am a creature.*
> *This is how God made me.*
> *It is good.*

I couldn't have known how much and how often I would need this prayer that year. I had forty-six undergraduates under my care. From getting locked out, to missing home, to boy troubles, to suicidal episodes, they seemed to have endless needs. I became haunted by a feeling of constant vigilance in a way I imagine is something like being a parent. I was always "on" and ready to be interrupted. Caring for other humans in any capacity is a test of our creatureliness; it makes us think we need to be endless, and it shows us that we are not.

I felt guilty caring for myself. I often tried to pretend like I didn't have a body, like I was a machine of love and responsibility whose batteries never ran out. I learned quickly (though not as quickly as I would have liked!) that ignoring my needs never worked because I have a body, and it makes its demands. What good did it do to give until I had nothing more to give? To be so wrung out that all I had to offer were the tired, dirty drippings of an overused kitchen towel (me)?

So, each week, I began to vigilantly guard one morning in which no one could bother me unless it was an absolute emergency. I slept in. I drove to a coffee shop in the next city so that no one would find me. I had an Americano with a ham-and-cheese croissant. I wrote in my journal. I listened to my music and had existential feelings. And then I returned to campus, wonderfully refreshed, ready to handle whatever the fourth floor of Horton Hall could give me.

I was able to be much more generous with others when I was more generous with myself. But it also began to unlock a secret suspicion in me: that my body was not a mere vehicle for good works, but a means of grace. My needs became a reminder to me that, as Julian of Norwich puts it: God made me, God loves me, God cares for me. My gnostic self saw faith as some special mystery separate from my body, but as I began to tend to myself more gently, I began to perceive that actually my body itself had a secret knowledge. That it spoke to me of the mysteries of God. That when I silenced it, I silenced God.

The early Christians spent a lot of time and ink emphasizing that Jesus really had a body. Gnosticism, escape from the body, is exactly the opposite of the message of Christianity. The good news of the Christian faith begins with this incomprehensible event: "The Word became flesh" (John 1:14). God did not rescue us from the world of bodies and sickness and death; He entered into it and began to redeem it from the inside out. In taking on a body, God declared that this world and these bodies are worth saving. I love the way Saint Athanasius (d. 373), that great defender of the incarnation, puts it:

> You know how it is when some great king enters a large city and dwells in one of its houses; because of his dwelling in that single house, the whole city is honored, and enemies and robbers cease to molest it. Even so is it with the King of all; He has come into our country and dwelt in one body amidst the many, and in consequence the designs of the enemy against mankind have been foiled and the corruption of death, which formerly held them in its power, has simply ceased to be. For the human race would have perished utterly had not the Lord and Savior of all, the Son of God, come among us to put an end to death.[1]

By taking on a body, God "honored," which here means "made honorable," our bodies and our fleshly world. Jesus didn't come to save us from our bodies; He came to save our bodies from sin and death. But we're so ingrained with this suspicion that our bodies are expendable, it can take a long time to understand that they are actually a means of grace.

That was how it was for Saint Augustine of Hippo (354–430). The North African bishop whose theology is unrivaled in its influence on the Western world had a very complex relationship with bodies. He rarely forgot that he had a body, and that was half the problem. Like any self-respecting

> **In taking on a body, God declared that this world and these bodies are worth saving.**

rebellious youth, prior to his conversion he spent his twenties experimenting with different religions, sleeping with his concubine, and reading depressing philosophy. Though he lived a hedonistic life, giving in to all the cravings of his body, he felt deeply conflicted. In a passage of *Confessions* (his spiritual autobiography), he describes his youth as one tossed by unruly desires, where "all around me hissed a cauldron of illicit loves."[2] Far from satisfying him, his carnal exploits left him only hungrier and more lustful than he began. Augustine went through many phases in an effort to reconcile his intellectual intuitions, his unruly desires, and moral discomfort: he flitted from an Epicurean hedonism (giving in to all desires!), to Stoicism (attempting to train one's desires), to Manichaeism (attempting to kill one's desires!). It was in this last phase that he remained longest before his conversion.

Originating as an offshoot of Christianity, Manichaeism was a gnostic cult that believed transcendence of bodily desires could be achieved through a series of complicated and mystical practices. Manichaeans were very serious about transcending the physical sphere of pleasures. They believed procreation was evil. Their priests only ate vegetables like cucumbers and melons, because they were perceived as less "physical" and more spiritual because you could see light through them. (I share this fact as often as I have the opportunity because I think it is very funny.) They sought, as much as possible, to sever ties with all that was physical, pleasurable, and bodily. As a man who had been deeply wounded by his own pursuit of pleasure, Augustine found this escape from the prison of his own desirous body appealing. And yet, it was through the beauty of the physical world that he would ultimately experience God's love and be converted. He puts it most beautifully in the following passage:

> Late have I loved you, beauty so old and so new: late have I loved you. And see, you were within and I was in the external world and sought you there, and in my unlovely state I plunged into those lovely created things which you made. You were with me and I was not with you. The lovely things kept me far from you, though if they did not have their existence in you, they had no existence at all. You called and cried out and shattered my deafness. You were radiant and resplendent, you put flight to my blindness. You were fragrant, and I drew in my breath and now pant after you. I taste you, and I feel but hunger and thirst for you. You touched me, and I am set on fire to attain the peace which is yours.[3]

Notice all the sensual language he uses: sound, fragrance, taste, touch. These bodily things, which at first left him hungry and alone, were transfigured in Christ, so that he sensed God's hand upholding the good creation in which He delights, shining through it and beckoning Augustine to dive further and further into the beauty so ancient and so new. Augustine never entirely resolved his discomfort with bodies, but he stopped trying to escape his, for it was through it and all its unruly desires that he began to perceive the transformative grace of Christ, which does not rescue us from our bodies but transforms them.

I think my favorite early Christian writing on the goodness of bodies is *On the Soul and the Resurrection* by Gregory of Nyssa. In it, Gregory records his conversation with his sister Macrina on her deathbed. Gregory is deeply anguished at the idea of losing his sister, who raised and educated him, and so he begins to ask her about the soul, and how the soul will outlast the body. In the moment when her body is failing her, you might think she would opine on spiritual blessings, but instead, what we find is a gradual argument for the hope of resurrected bodies.

With the gentleness and compassion of a big sister, she speaks of human beings as creaturely and embodied beings who are always incomplete in themselves, and are, therefore, always drawn toward various needs, be those for food, sex, or companionship. She points out that this reflects our shared nature with animals. Far from being something negative, Macrina sees our creatureliness as a design feature, God constantly drawing us back to himself. These bodies of ours remind us of a precious truth: we are contingent beings. We did not have to exist, but we do. We are dependent upon others for our continued existence, and more fundamentally, we are dependent on God. As the psalmist puts it, "It is He who has made us, and not we ourselves; we are His people and the sheep of His pasture" (Psalm 100:3 NASB). Even as she languishes in a dying body, she is reminded of her complete dependence on God. That all the needs of her tender self recall her back to God. Macrina asks Gregory that if our bodily need were "altogether rooted out . . . what is there which would raise us toward union with the heavenly? Or if love is taken away, in what manner will we be joined with the Divine?"[4]

When I finally started treating my body as less than expendable, I began to see what Macrina meant. Bodies are good. Their needs reflect our total dependence on God, and God's total love of and provision for us. It is not in spite of our bodies that we experience God, but through them. Lately, every time I feel hungry or sleepy, I think to myself, *I am God's sheep. He cares for me.* But I still have much to learn. How much gentler and freer would I be if every time I needed something—sleep, food, solitude—I experienced it as a reminder that God loves me?

You Are Not a Machine

The metaphors we use to describe ourselves matter. I've noticed that we often talk about ourselves like we're machines. We "adjust." We "process" life events. We "recharge our batteries" when we're worn out. On their own, these metaphors might be harmless enough, but when they become ingrained in our self-imagination, they can become destructive. We act like we should be able to expect the same things from ourselves every day. We demand consistency; we are hard on ourselves when we don't perform, function, work. Machines work and so should we. When machines break, we throw the useless things away, or melt them down for parts.

You are not a machine. You are more like a garden. You need different things on different days, a little more sun today, a little less water tomorrow. You have fallow and fruitful seasons. This is not a design flaw; it is wiser than perpetual sameness. If you expect a garden to "produce" things with the same regularity and consistency as a machine, you will be disappointed. If you try to maintain a garden the same way you would a machine, you will destroy it. The same is true of your body and emotional life.

What does your garden need today? This morning mine needed solitude and enough sleep. Then it needed a cup of sweet, hot tea before the world was awake. It needed to pay attention to the daffodils blooming dutifully on my desk, to watch raindrops stroll in little rivulets down my window, and to listen to Yo-Yo Ma play a Bach cello suite. Perhaps you will say that *need* is too strong a word, but I would reply that perhaps you have not listened to *Cello Suite no. 2 in D Minor*. I felt a need for it like a physical hunger in my body.

People call this self-care, but I think there's something more. "Self-care" implies that I, my "self," am capable of caring for myself. And in a way I am, and that is good. But there's also something else. When I pause to take care of myself, I acknowledge implicitly that the world will go on without me. That my "self" cannot do everything. That I am not God.

Self-care is a realization of the limits of the self.

Self-care is a realization of the limits of the self, a hearkening to the fundamentally contingent nature of being a human. It is not closed in a little bubble of selfishness, but a gentle, trusting acknowledgment that God is God and I am not. When you rest, you tell the truth about the world.

Forgetting you have a body is not heroism; it is hubris. If you neglect your bodily needs, you will find yourself pouting in Paris, or under a bush in Beersheba telling God you wish you were dead. You should take care of yourself because it will make you a more stable person, more able to function usefully in the world, more capable of helping and encouraging other people. But you should also care for yourself because you are not God; you are His creature, and He delights in showing His love for you. Your physical needs are a daily, hourly reminder that God didn't create you to be alone, desperate, and hungry, but to be tended to. Like a happy, plump sheep.

When I get too full of myself and think I can rule the world without taking a nap or having a snack, I read Psalm 131:

> My heart is not proud, LORD,
>   my eyes are not haughty;
> I do not concern myself with great matters
>   or things too wonderful for me.
> But I have calmed and quieted myself,
>   I am like a weaned child with its mother;
>   like a weaned child I am content.
> Israel, put your hope in the LORD
>   both now and forevermore.

I love this psalm. It is so intimate and personal, recalling that most visceral sense of safety and physical comfort: being rocked in a mother's arms. This is where we all begin, in total dependence. Each one of us exists today because someone fed and changed us as babies. I love that the psalmist asks us to imagine God as a mother, gently caring for our needs. It is precious to me, and I have sometimes needed to know God as my mother too.

So, today I remember that I have a body. And that it is a very, very good thing.

To Read

"Wild Geese" by Mary Oliver

On the Incarnation by Saint Athanasius

To See

The Annunciation by Henry Ossawa Tanner

To Listen

"Just Before Dawn" by Sonnymoon

To Ponder

These artworks all focus on the integrity, goodness, and holiness of the body. Mary Oliver's poem and Sonnymoon's eerie song remind us of the essential neediness of human beings, our creatureliness, and Athanasius's book reminds us that this creatureliness is good, made honorable by Jesus. Henry Ossawa Tanner's image reminds us of the simplicity, humility, and humanness of Mary the mother of Jesus. And yet it was precisely through her humanity, her embodiment, that Jesus was born; not despite her body, but because of it.

How do you regard your body? Do you think of faith as an attainment of "secret knowledge" that is more important than your body? Listen to your body and ask what it might have to tell you about God.

4

Enjoy things unironically

He had garnished his soul in the subtlest taste and now he longed
for the old rubbish.

—F. Scott Fitzgerald, *The Beautiful and the Damned*

My brother Nathan has a Facebook discussion group called
"The Overthinkers," where participants overthink a variety
of topics ranging from plot holes in the *Lord of the Rings* to
the theological aporia of free will, to the arbitrary phonetic
rules of the English language. It's a lot of fun. The other day,
Nathan asked, "What is your guilty pleasure?" The answers
and ensuing discussion perplexed and mildly infuriated me.
One person said their guilty pleasure was audiobooks; a second answered that it was M. Night Shyamalan's film *The
Village*; while yet another individual replied, "the 1995 BBC
adaptation of *Pride and Prejudice*." *I'm sorry*, I thought as I
scrolled through the answers, *it must be so embarrassing for*

you to like self-improvement, an Academy Award–nominated film, and the best adaptation of a classic regency-era novel. In what upside-down planet were these pleasures one ought to feel guilty about?

Full disclosure: I might have been a *bit* sore because I guilelessly replied, "The Netflix reality shows *Love Is Blind* and *Indian Matchmaking*" before I read any of the other replies. I like to think my enjoyment of these off-brand reality shows is because I'm "researching" the "human condition" for my "future novel." Does the fact that I'm single and in my midtwenties have anything to do with my enjoyment of these things? I offer no comment.

When the hot bluster of my incredulity cooled, I began to ponder what dynamics were at work in this puzzling discussion. There are certainly pleasures one ought to feel guilty about, habits that harm other people or our own moral character. But usually when we ask someone about their guilty pleasures, we mean fairly innocent pastimes about which they feel embarrassment or shame because they're too simple, gauche, or shallow. Why, then, would people profess embarrassment over what seem to me perfectly tasteful and respectable pleasures?

My inner cynic bitterly proposed that some of the commenters did *not* in fact feel embarrassed by these pleasures and had only used the post as a way to flaunt what good taste they had. This was, no doubt, the case for some. But most of the Overthinkers seemed earnest about their guilty pleasures; there was a discernible squirm in the tone of their confessional comments. This was all the more perplexing; how on earth had they come to regard these objectively good things as "guilty pleasures"? The more I thought about it, the more it seemed like people were simply talking about the things they liked, but that the very fact of liking them was a matter of discomfort, shame, or guilt. It wasn't the *object* of liking they felt guilty for; it was the *liking* itself.

Ah, I thought, *this I understand.*

I understand the shame associated with enjoying things, enjoying the wrong things, or enjoying them *too much*, because I have spent too much time on Twitter. I started to use Twitter more regularly during the first year of my PhD studies as one of the more entertaining ways to procrastinate on writing my thesis. Twitter really is an echo chamber. If you shout bitterness, anger, irony into the abyss, the abyss will shout back. If, instead, you shout weird literary jokes and your opinions about the best brand of black tea, random internet strangers will scream their favorite adaptations of *Pride and Prejudice* and lipstick brands back at you. It's great! In one sense, Twitter is a wonderful place to be an enthusiastic person who enjoys things. It's a perfect platform for discovering people who enjoy the same things you do, no matter how obscure.

However, it is also a place where people will find your corner of sunshine and obscure jokes about Charles Dickens, and become absolutely incensed by it.

For instance, once, after experimenting with bread baking during the 2020 lockdown, I tweeted that the way yeast makes bread rise seems almost magical. While the tweet garnered some positive responses from fellow burgeoning quarantine bakers, a group of about a dozen grumpy men digitally dog-piled the tweet, sending me angry emojis, saying I was obnoxious, blocking me, and intimating that my awe regarding the remarkable properties of yeast had a more sinister monetary goal.

(Let me assure you that, to my great disappointment, I do not have a secret bread-baking business, and am, in no way, financially benefited by the sale of yeast. Alas!)

I was mostly unfazed, accustomed as I am to the lunacy of the internet, but I was genuinely curious about why they hated this particular tweet *so much*. With the cool indifference of a researcher, I asked several of them why they were mad. It seemed that my crime was that I enjoyed baking too much, that it was irritating, and that it would be preferable if I were more chill. One of them asked me if I could "not be this way." I replied that, regrettably, I could not.

No wonder people are reticent to admit pleasures in life!

I find the way we police our own and other people's enjoyment utterly fascinating. By nature, I am the opposite of the enjoyment police; you could call me an enjoyment anarchist. I tend to think that life is hard, and wherever we find innocent enjoyment, we should lap it up, suck the marrow out, and give thanks to God. But this is easier said than done. The hatred (and that is the right word) and accompanying guilt I have sometimes experienced for enjoying life, and admitting to enjoying it, has caused me to ponder why we have such a fraught relationship with pleasure, enjoyment, and liking things. We hedge our admissions of enjoyment in embarrassment and irony, and we assure ourselves that we don't indulge too often or too much.

Why do we do this? I cannot speak for the enjoyment police, but as far as I can tell, my own reticence to fully enjoy things boils down to three preoccupations:

Fear of what people will think of me.

Shame about feeling pleasure.

Guilt for enjoying things when the world is falling apart.

I think these are significant impediments to happiness that need to be addressed if we're going to live well. Admitting you like *Indian Matchmaking* might seem like a small thing, but the forces that make enjoying or admitting you enjoy things so fraught and complicated are the same ones that corrode your ability to form deep friendships, to believe in good things, and to admit with no hesitation that being alive is a good thing. It is my contention that the spiritual and emotional muscles we exercise in thoroughly and full-heartedly enjoying innocent pleasures are at the heart of living a good and meaningful life. To enjoy things unironically can be a small act of resistance to the soul-deadening forces of the modern world and can have profound spiritual repercussions.

> The spiritual and emotional muscles we exercise in thoroughly and full-heartedly enjoying innocent pleasures are at the heart of living a good and meaningful life.

Unconvinced? Let's explore the three obstacles that keep us from unironically liking things. To keep you hooked, I will confess (another) one of my own guilty pleasures at the end of this chapter.

What Will Other People Think of Me?

The first reason we deny or diminish our enjoyments is that we're afraid of what other people might think of us. This fear can take many forms. We might be afraid to admit how much we love *Avatar: The Last Airbender* because we don't want to seem silly, uncultured, stupid, or weird. Indeed, this fear might not only keep us from admitting our enjoyment, but might even prevent us from indulging our enjoyment to its fullest extent. Or perhaps we are afraid that if our Christian friends knew we like the English pop band The 1975, they might think that we're godless progressives with no standards of morality. Or perhaps we're afraid that if we admitted how much we like Bach, people might think we are uppity, pretentious snobs. Whether it be our taste, our morality, or our intelligence, we're afraid that admitting our enjoyment of a particular thing might communicate something that causes others to disapprove of us. Perhaps we aren't even afraid of *what* people will think of us, but merely that they *will* think something of us at all.

I think this speaks to a much deeper fear and desire, woven deeply into human nature. The reason what other people think of us is such a strong motivator of our behavior is that we are creatures made to thrive in relationship and community. Relationship is etched deep in our nature. As members of the animal kingdom, we need approval from others as a primal matter of survival; if no one likes me, who will protect me? Provide for me? Help me if I fall down? As social animals, we need approval from others to help determine the meaning of our actions and the worth of our lives. If no one likes me, to whom will I belong? How will I know my work matters? And as spiritual beings made in the image of God, our very existence is tucked into the eternal reciprocity of the Trinity.

We are made for relationship and union; any threat to that feels enormous. The fear of isolation nags at us so deeply that we would do almost anything to prevent it. We adjust our enjoyments, deny our personalities, and fashion ourselves into the sort of people who will not rock the boat, who can belong and be accepted. Caring about what other people think about us is not necessarily a bad thing. Indeed, it is responsible for much of the growth in our lives. There can be positive side effects of this fear when we *try* to like things because we think other people will think well of us if we do. I have discovered and come to love some beautiful books, music, and foods I would not otherwise have enjoyed, because someone I admired liked them. I wanted to be like them, so I tried new things, and my intellect and enjoyment grew as a result.

But as with many of the most powerful things in life, there is a great danger too. If we severely curb who we are and what we enjoy to avoid rejection, we may end up actualizing the thing we fear most. By assuming that people couldn't like us as we are, and fashioning ourselves into something different, we execute our own self-rejection. By suppressing who you are, you may end up socially accepted in a group of people with whom you actually share very little in common, and who do not actually know you. To be accepted but not authentically known is, in my experience, a much more profound isolation than being honestly who you are, and lonely.

How then do we solve the mystery of wanting to be known, but also accepted?

In *The Four Loves* C. S. Lewis writes, "Friendship must be about something, even if it were only an enthusiasm for dominoes or white mice. Those who have nothing can share nothing; those who are going nowhere can have no fellow-travellers."[1] This has proven true for me. Some of my most treasured friendships have begun with the initial spark of mutual enjoyment, the disclosure of a "guilty pleasure," and the deep delight of discovering someone else is as obsessed as you.

I will never forget realizing Elena, my college roommate, was a kindred spirit. We were sitting in the humid canopy of a wedding tent on a sweltering August day for an induction dinner for new university students and their parents. As the business-casual-clad representatives droned on about academic achievements, employment rates, and denominational affiliations, Elena and I conspiratorially whispered over plates of wilting salad to ward off death by boredom or heatstroke. It was an odd trinity that first brought us together: *Anne of Green Gables*, Christopher Nolan, and *Lord of the Rings*. We effused. We overanalyzed. We speculated.

Thus sparked a long friendship of thinking too hard about the art we love.

Though our friendship has deepened beyond merely enjoying the same things, it is that rhythm of enjoying, recommending, and overanalyzing the things we love together that is still a central delight in our relationship. I like to think our taste has improved, but if it has, it is in no small part because we shamelessly enjoyed things thoroughly together.

Enjoyment gives us something for our friendships to be about other than our own fathomless need for connection. We find it easier to be our most generous and delightful selves when we are thinking about how much we love *Doctor Who* or birdwatching than when we are trying very hard to be a likeable person. And our connections with others will be much more profound if they are based on an honest disclosure of what we love in life, rather than a controlled image we present of ourselves to gain approval.

Addressing the fear of rejection by admitting our enjoyments and pleasures in life may seem a small and insignificant thing, but it is an honest beginning. A happiness built on the fragile foundation of other people's opinions about us is one bound to fail. Unabashedly liking something, and even admitting you like it, is a small practice in being who you are and offering it to others as a gift. Owning what you like and enjoy is an act of vulnerability, which invites connection. As you stretch your muscle in this area, you will be attuned to the other ways in which you curtail who you are and thus miss the intimacy of truly being known.

So, I dare you: tell someone your real guilty pleasure. They just might say, "Me too!"

The Tiny Puritan

The second thing that keeps us from unironically liking things is that we have a hidden suspicion that pleasure, desire, enjoying things is actually bad.

I like to describe this as the tyranny of the Tiny Puritan.

I am convinced that most of us have a Tiny Puritan who lives in our heads. He tells us it is his job to keep us from sinning. The Tiny Puritan sees all pleasure as temptation. He thinks the safest way to stay morally pure is to be chronically wary of one's own enjoyment, one's happiness, one's own heart. So when we find ourselves enjoying something (be it a particularly ripe peach, an amazing piece of music, or a first kiss), he makes a great fuss, furrowing his brows, grumbling, "Sinner! Be careful! You might get carried away!" The Tiny Puritan is a nuisance, but we're afraid to get rid of him, because we really do want to be good. Sometimes, we quietly admit to ourselves that we wish we could simply enjoy something, anything, without that hovering, vague cloud of shame. But he's just keeping us safe! How dare you question him?

The Tiny Puritan believes that all pleasures are guilty pleasures. Did you really enjoy that movie? The Tiny Puritan suggests you could/should be doing something more productive or spiritual. Did you absolutely love those donuts? The Tiny Puritan suggests that you are a glutton. Really like that novel? The Tiny Puritan reminds you that people are dying in a country that you don't otherwise care about, and that you are both hard-hearted and undisciplined in your use of time.

We all handle the Tiny Puritan in our own special way. Some people learn early in life to lock the Tiny Puritan in a box and bury him somewhere deep in their subconscious, boldly enjoying pleasures both innocent and salacious, only occasionally hearing echoes of his baleful scream. Some of us try to bargain with the Tiny Puritan ("This really is a very innocent pleasure, good sir! And I fully intend to do something Selfless and Meaningful later tonight!"), enjoying some small pleasures, but not without being flattened slightly by his derisive scoff. He defeats some of us. We end up trying to follow all the Puritan's demanding rules, just so he'll shut up. We don't enjoy many things very thoroughly, but at least we don't feel awash in shame all the time.

It reminds me of one of my favorite films: *Babette's Feast*.

The 1980s Danish film follows the life of two sisters (Martine and Filippa), the children of a sincere but austere Lutheran pastor, who live a strict and pleasureless life on a barren and remote coast of Jutland. Each, in their turn, falls in love but turns the suitor down out of a misguided sense of duty and piety. They justify their self-denial as a triumph over worldly temptation, but regret haunts their quiet moments. After their father dies, they do their best to tend to his dwindling congregation. Out of the long wasteland of their lives comes Babette, a refugee from France. Babette brings life and beauty to the dour daily grind of the sisters—simple pleasures, good food, flowers in the window. After many years, Babette wins the lottery and resolves to move back to France, but before she does, she has one request: that she might cook a feast for the sisters and their friends. Though circumspect, they accept.

Babette embarks on a conspiracy of excess. She sends her nephew on a mission to procure special ingredients—fish, fruit, wine, even a turtle. Like Lady Wisdom in Proverbs, she sets her table beautifully, mixes her wines, and prepares a feast unlike anything the self-denying Jutlanders have ever seen. The sisters watch in horror, trying to decide whether they should abstain from Babette's extravagance or indulge in her sumptuous feast.

When the night of the feast comes, the sisters and the old villagers attend the feast but privately agree not to talk about the food. Only one guest truly appreciates the greatness of Babette's feast: Lorens, an experienced general and man of the world, the former suitor of Martine. With each course, he becomes more incredulous—the finest wines, the most succulent dishes, the most exotic ingredients. A true connoisseur, he appreciates every facet of the feast, each carefully curated morsel, and cannot understand how the guests around him seem bent on ignoring the sensuous masterpiece unfolding before them. They have been given pure grace, a work of generosity, needing nothing of them other than enjoyment, but they treat it as temptation.

Try as they might to be somber and indifferent to the beauty and bounty of Babette's table, the guests begin to experience a transformation. Old pettiness is confronted and resolved in magnanimity. Shameful sins are confessed and forgiven. Love is rekindled. Their best attempts at severity dissolve beneath the entrancing power of Babette's generosity, and the evening ends with all the guests rejoicing together beneath a canopy of stars. It is revealed that Babette has spent all her money on the feast, and that she will stay in Jutland after all. Martine and Filippa are penitent for their lack of enjoyment, Martine sobbing, "Now you will be poor the rest of your life." Babette simply responds, "An artist is never poor." Babette knew what the sisters did not, that God's world is a gift of grace, that God is the artist who is always pleased with His good work, and that we honor Him by loving and enjoying His good gifts.

> **God invites us to taste His love in every perfect apple pie, to feel our souls brush infinity in the consolation of human love, to be drawn through music into worship.**

I sometimes wonder how often we have been like the suspicious Jutlanders, silencing the voice of God because we are afraid to let Him speak to us in our delight. God has set a feast for us in the world. He invites us to taste His love in every perfect apple pie, to feel our souls brush infinity in the consolation of human love, to be drawn through music into worship. In each generous pleasure, each plucking of the strings of desire in our heart, the Holy Spirit whispers of the new creation to us. Will we listen, or turn away in fear?

So, I dare you to take great pleasure in things. Tell the Tiny Puritan to get lost. Eat the feast.

How Can I Enjoy Things When the World Is Burning?

This is the final hurdle: we feel guilty enjoying things because the world is falling apart.

This often manifests itself in two forms: the Social Justice Sadist and the Benighted Cynic. Both suffer from the misplaced conviction that it is a moral obligation to binge-watch the world burn. They think it is more adult, rational, moral, and compassionate to watch the news than to re-watch the Megan Follows adaptation of *Anne of Green Gables* for the fifty-seventh time, or to bake a cake. I am not at all convinced that this is the case. Especially because, in my experience, binge-watching the dumpster fire of the world does one of two things, both of which are spectacularly useless: it makes us mush or it makes us hard. In the first case, you become a catatonic mush of useless anxiety and hypervigilance. Unable to rip your eyes away from the vast dreadfulness of the world, you become an informed moral paraplegic: aware but frozen. Of course, the even greater danger is becoming hardened, a person who is not surprised by anything. You are cynical, knowing, inured to the cruelty of the world. When you watch sweet things, you call them corny, cheesy, saccharine, or some other culinary epithet because you know better than to believe there's actually goodness in the world. You have gazed into the abyss, and it has gazed back.

These are two sides of the same coin: helplessness.

The world is too big for us to save, and this is very upsetting. We wish we could do something, and we do our best in our own small ways, but there is a vastness to the need, and a profundity to the brokenness that we cannot, in our own strength, extinguish. Perhaps we derive some sense of accomplishment as we rehearse our hatred of political enemies, tweet with pithy indignation, and lock our phones at 11:45 p.m., having read another depressing news story. We feel like involved and informed citizens. But realistically, the amount of time we spend doomscrolling is not commensurate with our positive contribution to the welfare of society. And on the other hand, our catatonic dread of imminent environmental catastrophe neither makes the world better, nor does it enable us to be helpful or useful to our neighbor. No one ever needs to remind us that the world is broken; we know it deep in our bones. What we need is a reason to keep trying to make it whole.

I am not saying that we should all bury our heads in the sand and be desensitized to the suffering of our fellow man. Far from it! The desire for wholeness and justice is one of the most natural, humane, and honest feelings that we have. It is good that we are concerned for the welfare of our world and our neighbor; to recognize the reciprocal fragility of our existence is the beginning of much good. But somewhere in this good concern, a pernicious lie needles its way in. We begin to think that the war with evil means constant eye contact with it. That we must be constantly vigilant, somber, and righteously indignant. That enjoying innocent pleasures is criminally insensitive, hard-hearted, escapist. That it is not morally licit for us to enjoy anything until the world is completely just, whole, and right.

Let's explore this idea.

Let us imagine that you manage to forgo the indulgence of tragedy rubbernecking, you delete all your social media profiles, you forgo the helplessness of dumpster-fire spectatorship, and you devote yourself completely to the eradication of some evil in the world. You are determined, in short, not to enjoy any simple joys until every person on earth can enjoy simple joys. You run into several problems. First, you cannot always be saving the world; it is a practical impossibility to always be saving the world. You must sometimes sleep or eat (see previous chapter). And there's much mundanity even in the noblest of professions, many empty moments of waiting, long pauses between great bursts of effort. What will you do in these lulls? Stare at the wall and contemplate your privilege? Read yet another depressing article? Do either of these options actually benefit the people around you? I should say that you would be very boring at parties, but of course you probably wouldn't attend parties, so the point is moot. My point is that even a life marked by a diligent pursuit of justice will occasionally have empty moments which you might as well fill with innocent pleasures, which will elevate your own happiness and that of those around you. Watch *Anne of Green Gables*. It's fine.

But I think we can go further than this.

There is a lopsidedness to a life whose only aim is the destruction of evil. Our horror at injustice and suffering gestures to our intuitive sense that life is meant to be good, enjoyed, not lived in desperation. We grieve hunger because people should be filled with good food, not because good food is bad. We weep with those who weep because we wish that someday they might be able to laugh again. To focus on the brokenness and wickedness of the world puts at the center of our moral world not justice, kindness, and truth, but injustice, suffering, and incredulity. Jack Gilbert puts it bluntly: "To make injustice the only measure of our attention is to praise the Devil."[2]

C. S. Lewis provides some very helpful advice on this point in his excellent little sermon "Learning in War-Time":

> We may have a duty to rescue a drowning man, and perhaps, if we live on a dangerous coast, to learn life-saving so as to be ready for any drowning man when he turns up. It may be our duty to lose our own lives in saving him. But if anyone devoted himself to life-saving in the sense of giving it his total attention—so that he thought and spoke of nothing else and demanded the cessation of all other human activities until everyone had learned to swim—he would be a monomaniac. The rescue of drowning men is, then, a duty worth dying for, but not worth living for.[3]

In all our efforts to save the world, it is easy to lose sight of the fact that it is a world worth saving. It is a world with pad Thai and first kisses and perfectly tiny puppy dogs. It is a world with fields of daffodils in the spring and crystalline perfection in the winter. It is a world with the unbridled glee of a child who has learned how to tell a joke. It is a world that didn't have to exist but does and is inexplicably wonderful. I am convinced that the joy and goodness of the world are more fundamental than its brokenness. Only when we are awake to the extravagant, unnecessary gift that it is can we be fully energized to protect it. We should fight for justice, for others and ourselves, because we want everyone to have a beautiful, gentle life.

The idea that despite all evidence to the contrary, goodness, light, and beauty are more fundamental than the evil, sickness, and pain that would seek to destroy them is a theme which pervades *The Lord of the Rings*. *The Return of the King* is a desperate book, always on the cusp of defeat, and yet it is shot through with the conviction that goodness outlasts evil. The following appears during the most hopeless moments of Sam and Frodo's passage through Mordor, as they approach what will surely be their own demise. Yet even in this long defeat, there is hope:

> There, peeping among the cloud-wrack above a dark tor high up in the mountains, Sam saw a white star twinkle for a while. The beauty of it smote his heart, as he looked up out of the forsaken land, and hope returned to him. For like a shaft, clear and cold, the thought pierced him that in the end the Shadow was only a small and passing thing: there was light and high beauty for ever beyond its reach.[4]

There is a scene in Peter Jackson's *Lord of the Rings* so wonderful that I shall forgive its not being in the books. Sam and Frodo are trudging through the depths of Mordor, parched, hungry, and exhausted. Ravaged by months of travel and the dark influence of the Ring, Frodo is tormented by despair. It seems like they can go no farther. Sam says to Frodo:

> "Do you remember the Shire, Mr. Frodo? It'll be spring soon. And the orchards will be in blossom. And the birds will be nesting in the hazel thicket. And they'll be sowing the summer barley in the lower fields . . . and eating the first of the strawberries with cream. Do you remember the taste of strawberries?"

Frodo cannot remember strawberries, or springtime. The darkness clings to him and he cannot see ahead. But something in Sam is strengthened.

"Then let us be rid of it . . . once and for all! Come on, Mr. Frodo. I can't carry it for you . . . but I can carry you!"[5]

It is not some great intellectual argument that gives Sam the power to climb the mountain. It is not some grand moral conviction that gives him strength to carry Frodo. The memory of a simple pleasure and an uncomplicated joy parts the thick smoke of Mordor's despair and reminds Sam that there is sweetness, and goodness, and innocence, a life worth fighting for.

When I was younger and had been less battered by the world, I used to think Paul's words to the Philippians were a kind of sanctified escapism: "Whatever is true, whatever is noble, whatever is right, whatever is pure, whatever is lovely, whatever is admirable—if anything is excellent or praiseworthy—think about such things" (Philippians 4:8). Now that I am older, I realize I do not need to be reminded that the world is dark and difficult; I am well aware, and very tired. What I need is a vision of goodness so bright that it lights the path ahead of me, keeps me faithful, and makes me brave. So enjoy things thoroughly, because the memory of strawberries may just give you the strength you need to defeat Sauron.

My Guilty Pleasure

Ostensibly, this chapter was about guilty pleasures.

So let me confess my most recent one to you: BTS.

For the unfortunate souls among you for whom these three letters ring no bells, let me enlighten you. BTS is a Korean boy band composed of seven perfectly coiffed members. The three letters stand for a Korean phrase that when translated means

"Bulletproof Boy Scouts," which is *so endearingly adorable.* They are, as one of my friends would say, "Big Happy"; their performances are an adrenaline rush dressed in pastel high fashion, with a fast-beating heart of joy at being alive. The real BTS experience is not merely listening but watching; their showmanship, dancing, and fashion are remarkable. Oh, the skill! The joy! How can you watch and not be glad to live on the same planet?

And the best of all? Their obvious friendship and celebration of each other.

Now, why might I be tempted to regard my enjoyment of this band as "guilty pleasure"? Well, I might be afraid of what people would think of me. I am an author, a scholar! I have a reputation to protect! Might this enjoyment separate me from my peers, make me seem silly and unserious?

I reply, first, that I've never seen a set of people quite so serious about their craft and, second, that BTS has provided fodder for friendship. After confessing this enjoyment to one friend, he enthusiastically burst out, "Did you know one of their albums is based on Jungian archetypes?" Since that's a topic in which we are both interested, this initiated a deep dive into the album and conjecture about whether they had read primary or secondary literature. You never know what good conversations and mutual delight a guilty pleasure confessed might enable!

Perhaps the Tiny Puritan might tell me that BTS really is a guilty pleasure, at best a frivolous waste of time and at worst a worldly celebration of hedonism and materialism.

To the Tiny Puritan I would reply that watching BTS reminds me that God didn't need to make the world, and that He didn't have to make it a place where harmonies and melodies would make our hearts feel like they'll explode out of our chests, or where our bodies can synchronize in the profound physical expression of emotion that dance affords, but God did. It is a wonderful world to live in, and the Lord did a good thing when He created both music and the members of BTS.

In a last-ditch effort, my own conscience asks: is it okay to enjoy Korean boy band BTS when the world is being engulfed in literal and metaphorical flames? When I watch BTS dance, I am reminded that we humans are made for so much more than sorrow and desperation and anger. We are capable of disciplined perfection, yes, and also utter, unspeakable joy. Watching BTS gloriously live into their skill reminds me of Jesus' words: "I came so that they would have life, and have it abundantly" (John 10:10 NASB). In the slog of ordinary life, it is difficult to imagine what this might mean, but the pure, happy energy of BTS is a small icon of the "Big Happy" for which we are made.

It's a strawberry on Mount Doom.

So, in the end, here is my verdict for enjoyment of BTS: not guilty.

Now that we've got all that out of the way, tell me: what is your guilty pleasure?

To Read

"Learning in War-Time" by C. S. Lewis

To See

Babette's Feast (1987)

To Listen

"Dynamite" by BTS

"Sincerity Is Scary" by The 1975

To Ponder

I chose these artworks to help you feel less guilty about experiencing enjoyment. Lewis's essay tells us that to enjoy things even when the world is falling to pieces is essentially human, *Babette's Feast* reminds us that desire is simply divine, and BTS shows us that life is worth enjoying.

What keeps you from enjoying things? Pick one thing you know to be an innocent pleasure. Enjoy it thoroughly, and then share that joy with someone else.

What are your metaphorical "strawberries" on Mount Doom? Do something today to remind yourself of the "light and high beauty" at the heart of reality.

5

Tell yourself a good story

I can only answer the question "What am I to do?" if I can answer
the prior question "Of what story or stories do I find myself a part?"

—Alasdair MacIntyre, *After Virtue*

"You must have at least three more bites," I said in my best
attempt at sounding authoritative.

Lilian, my two-year-old niece, considered this demand, gaz-
ing contemplatively at a mosaic of orange rice, pomegranate
seeds, and cheese on her plate. The cogs, I could tell, were
turning. After a few moments, she selected one, exactly one,
pomegranate seed, and popped it into her mouth.

"I suppose that counts for one bite," I said to myself more
than Lilian, "but I see now that I should have been more specific."

I was quarantining at my sister Sarah's house upon reentry
to the United Kingdom during the pandemic. It was one of
those moments when life's inevitable inconveniences happen

to bring a gift: two perfect weeks utterly devoted to sister and auntie time. I set aside the final edits for my PhD thesis, which I knew would swamp me soon enough. We baked many cookies, watched BBC miniseries, and talked about absolutely everything. Amongst my purer motives, one of the goals for the stay was to install myself as a beloved auntie in the memory of my namesake niece. Endearing oneself to a toddler, however, is no mission for the faint of heart. One must be an endless font of entertainment, ready to transform into a "horsey" at any moment, and possess a strong intuition as a translator for any attempts with the raw materials of language. At that particular moment, I was sitting with Lilian while my nephew napped, trying to extend lunch as long as possible to grant my sister a few precious minutes alone. The goal of extending lunchtime was frustrated by the fact that Lilian simply didn't seem interested in eating.

Suddenly, I had an idea. "Shall I tell you a story, Lilian?"

She nodded in a sideways motion and made a sound of affirmation. She is prone to affirm questions even when she is not quite sure what they mean; she likes to seem in the know. I took advantage of this impulse and launched into the first story I could think of, *Cinderella*.

"Once upon a time . . ." I began as Lilian selected a lonely grain of rice to eat. I edited and embellished as I went, making much of the mice that were Cinderella's friends, and, suffering from a twinge of feminist guilt about the choice of story, emphasizing that cinders could never conceal the beauty of a good heart. Lilian listened, apparently contented, occasionally deigning to eat another piece of rice. I found myself stumbling over how to make this a moral story about how character matters more than appearances, and what sort of thing a fairy godmother is, which Lilian seemed to accept with equanimity. As I went, the story began to pick up speed, and I began to feel in myself the rhythms of its tensions and resolutions, its moments of revelation and unveiling, its fairy tale delights, its wonderful strangeness. When I reached "and they lived happily ever after," I felt quite satisfied, as an auntie and a storyteller.

A moment of silence transpired. Lilian speared the slice of Port Salut on the plate with her forefinger, blinked meaningfully, and petitioned: "Mowah?" (Translation: more).

When a two-year-old is quiet, happy, and consuming healthy foods, one seeks to extend the state as long as possible. So, on I went. After a few more fairy tales, I decided to try some Bible and saint stories. I told her about Saint Francis preaching to the birds, the Desert Father and his disobedient pitcher, Balaam and his talking donkey, Mary and her beautiful hymn. On and on we went, her uncharacteristic silence punctuated by interjections of "Mowah?" Eventually, I reached a point of desperation, having told every story I could think of (even part of *Lord of the Rings!*). Then, I had another idea.

"Once upon a time there was a little girl called Lilian," I began.

Her eyes widened in surprise.

"A lil gurl lala?"

"Yes." I nodded. "A little girl named Lilian. She lived in a house near the beautiful Downs, and one day she met a bunny who needed her help . . ."

The story came naturally, like a beautiful song I'd always loved but hadn't sung in a long time. From some deep subconscious well where every Beatrix Potter and Brambly Hedge tale had buried themselves, I found a bunny king, and a wounded paw, and a feast of dandelion wine and blackberry pies under the hill in the halls of the warren. Lilian listened, transfixed, her attention keener than it had been. When I reached the end, she was quiet for a moment.

"Lil gurl Lala?" she queried, just to make sure.

"Yes," I said, "a little girl named Lilian. Just like you."

"And Mama? And Fa? And Sa?"

A bright grin spread across her face. A story where real people lived, her people. This knowledge was too wonderful for Lilian; she could eat no more. But to her surprise, and my delight, forty minutes had passed, and her plate was clean. (Well, almost). A success by every measure!

Thus began a cherished ritual between "Lala" and me: funny, happy stories. Lilian developed an appetite for stories as voracious as her enjoyment of cheese (she is her auntie's niece, to be sure). At the end of meals, she would look at me expectantly: "Funny happy story?" she would ask, and I would tell them till I was almost dead. Certain stories became particularly beloved, but there was something particularly wonderful in "Lala stories." As I told them, I found myself visiting some of my first and foggiest memories. I had severe asthma as a child, and each night my mother would run a hot shower and sit with me in the steam telling me "Joy stories" until the humidity unstuck my swampy lungs and I could breathe again. Perhaps this is why stories have always felt like oxygen to me. And as I told story after story to this niece I love, I wondered if perhaps we all need someone who loves us to tell us stories to bring our souls to life.

One day during my quarantine, Lilian pattered into the living room holding a card with a portrait on it.

"Who dis, Mama?" she asked, presenting the card to my sister. Sarah scooped Lilian into her lap and held the postcard in her hands, where they could examine it together. It was a Christmas card from Gwennie, my mother's best friend. Gwennie has been one of the important characters in my story. Though not related to us by blood, for as long as I can remember, she has been a fixture in our family tree. It's hard to say how much she means to me. She came every year right before New Year's for a "Gwennie Christmas," and I used to stay at her house when my mother would go on speaking engagements. She is our chosen family, and it was almost unimaginable for Lilian not to recognize her immediately. But, of course, Lilian has only been on this planet for two years, and one of them was during a pandemic, when Gwennie was across the ocean.

Perhaps we all need someone who loves us to tell us stories to bring our souls to life.

Sarah drew her finger gently over the beloved face.

"This is Gwennie. She's one of our people. We love her."

This little moment stole my breath. Here was storytelling come to life. Sarah was helping Lilian understand the story in which she was living, introducing her to one of its best characters. To Lilian this was entirely natural and comforting. Lilian accepted it with as much enthusiasm as when I told her about fairy godmothers and bunny kings and talking donkeys. This was another "Lala story," and she was interested in hearing more.

"Once upon a time, there was a little girl called Lilian. She lived in a house in the hills. She was very loved, by Mama and

Fa, by Queen and Papa and all her aunties and uncles. And Gwennie loves her too."

What a good story.

The Sitcom of Life

Recently, it struck me that I enjoy stories as frequently as I eat food (which is to say, very consistently! Food and stories are both great!). On my bedside table, there is an unruly pile of books: a novel (a reread), a collection of short stories (riveting!), a travel book (a genre I've recently discovered I love), and a Bible. When I can't sleep (often), I pick up one and read till my eyes grow weary. I have two audiobooks going at any given time. And then there are the Netflix series. Right now I'm working my way through a legal drama, but I'm not always so sophisticated; more often than not it is something that makes me laugh, something about a plucky young heroine overcoming odds and discovering romance and/or literary success (yes, I'm fully aware this is wish fulfillment). My consumption of stories is somewhat compulsive, but I think it is a compulsion most people share to at least some extent.

From news to Netflix to novels, we surround ourselves with stories.

And we tell them too.

You may not think you're a storyteller, but when someone asks, "How are you?" all of us instinctively begin to spin a story. We don't usually list bullet points of events and outcomes; we tell the story of our day, stringing each event along a temporal string, each moment of suspense, tension, resolution, humor, or excitement another pearl on the strand. As a particularly striking example of this, I always think of a friend of mine in grad school who described her life as "the sitcom." I would come back to my dorm room (which I rarely locked), to find her sitting on my overstuffed chair ensconced in my crocheted blanket. "You'll never believe what happened on the sitcom today." A riveting description of her day told as an absurdist situational comedy flecked with twenty-something pathos inevitably followed. We named the recurring characters "coffee shop crush," "shift dictator," "the bonnie laird." When the well-known villain appeared, I'd shake my head knowingly and mutter, "Oh *her* again," and when there was a new installment in the ongoing love saga with the coffee shop crush who didn't know she existed, I leaned in, breathless.

We don't live in the same place anymore, but the sitcom is ongoing. When we catch up over FaceTime and learn that something particularly ridiculous has happened to either of us (as it often does), we'll knowingly roll our eyes and say, "The sitcom writers have really gone off the rails this year."

The stories we tell about our days become the stories we tell about our lives. We develop a habit of telling our stories that casts a mood, an ethos, an Instagram filter over how we see our lives, and how we invite others to see us.

I have two friends who have practiced telling themselves very different stories.

One of them has had an objectively difficult life. Her parents divorced when she was young, and she grew up tossed between an unstable, narcissistic parent and a parent too grieved to know what to do with her. Her young years were haunted by loss and trauma—untimely deaths, car wrecks, interpersonal cruelty, and illness. And yet, somehow, she talks about being lucky. To have found Jesus. To have fallen in love with a good man. To raise two beautiful children. Not long ago, she was diagnosed with terminal cancer. I sat in her living room, and we cried together over a cup of tea. But, somehow, even as she was staring death in the face, she still saw her story as a good one.

My other friend, at least from the outside, has a life many only dream of. His parents love each other, and they love him. He has been well provided for. He's successful and attractive, but somewhere in his life, he picked up the habit of telling himself a tragic story of being lonely, responsible, and forgotten. People need him, but don't see him; he just has to struggle through, not ask for help. He's very unhappy. Even as his life acquires more and more evidences of being successful, beautiful, beloved, he tells his story as one of gradual and complete loneliness.

With both of these friends, I have the distinct feeling that the stories they tell themselves and others about their lives are not, strictly speaking, the plain truth. The first friend died recently, and when she did, there was a part of me that couldn't accept her version of the story; it wasn't fair that someone so good and beautiful could be treated so unfairly by life so many times. I felt vicarious anger that she escaped a difficult childhood only to be taken out so young by cancer. And yet, who was I to question her experience? To tell her that her story was not a good one? Would I wish to steal that good story from her when so many other things had already been taken away? With the second friend, I felt conflicted. He wasn't delusional; I could see the moments that led him to such a bleak outlook. But I could also see that borders of his life were more generous and pleasant than he allowed himself to see. That he was loved and lucky.

116

It was not that the stories they told themselves were untrue; they each simply chose to turn the volume up on certain aspects of their storytelling, to put a filter over certain memories, to see some things more clearly, to put some things out of view entirely.

The stories we tell are not objective; they "make something" of our experiences, inclining us to notice some things and filter others out. The way we tell our stories gives our experiences a particular atmosphere, makes us think of ourselves as particular kinds of people. We tell ourselves stories to give our days, our years, and our lives a narrative arc. Narrative helps us string together the disparate experiences of our lives into a coherent whole. Stories are all about meaning, helping us place particular moments in the context of our other experiences so that we can understand them. Stories give us a sense of why things happened, and what might happen in the future. Stories help us know how to act in the world, what to do, and what to be afraid of.

Think of it this way: imagine if instead of telling Lilian that Gwennie is our person and we love her, Sarah had said "Gwennie is our enemy; we fear her." As a result of inhabiting that story, Lilian would interpret her experience of Gwennie differently. Where the good story would lead her to look for evidences of Gwennie's belovedness, the second story would lead her to view Gwennie with suspicion, her kindnesses regarded as manipulation, any ambiguous silences as signs of her malice. Gwennie would be as imperturbably wonderful as ever, but Lilian could not experience her that way. And that would be a real loss. And yet many of us experience a similar loss by getting caught in a bad story that we tell ourselves over and over again.

I know this because sometimes I tell myself a lonely story. I began telling myself this story in a stressful season when life called upon me to buckle down and take care of myself and tend to others. Due to a combination of circumstance and personality, I learned to survive for a while by creating a story where I was the responsible and forgotten friend. And it was a true story for a season, but it was only one book in the series of my life. By letting it harden into a permanent outlook, I allowed my thin, tired, gray story to make me much less helpful to the people for whom I imagined myself to be sacrificing. I could not see the generosity of others because my story had trained me only to see their needs. I couldn't experience the joy of relative stability and support because I had practiced seeing life as a situation that needed to be handled.

Many of us experience a similar loss by getting caught in a bad story that we tell ourselves over and over again.

The negative stories we tell ourselves are particularly powerful because they serve a purpose: they keep us safe. Negative stories keep us on guard; they teach us to see red, to anticipate loss, to rehearse tragedy. Even if they cast a deadening filter of gray over our lives, the sucker punch of thinking you're in a good, happy story—and then realizing suddenly and sickeningly that you are not—is so painful that we'd rather manage our expectations and tell a less beautiful story to begin with.

But the problem with these stories is that they don't make good on their promises. They don't stop bad things from happening; they keep us from being thankful for the good things that do. Bad stories train our eyes to look for loss, to rehearse tragedy, and in the process we begin to miss the fragile goodness of being alive. We don't want to face the reality that we don't have control over our lives; rain falls on the righteous and the wicked, cancer strikes the kind and the cruel, grace beyond measure visits those who notice it and those who disregard it.

What do we make of these tangled webs of lives we live? How do we weave a good story and not practice our own deception?

Becoming a Good Storyteller

I have recently come to love a book called *Piranesi* by Susanna Clarke. It has shown me that it is possible to be protected by the good stories we tell ourselves, as well as the bad ones. I don't want to spoil it because I want everyone to read it, but suffice it to say, it is about two characters who live in the same world. One of them tells himself a beautiful story, a story in which he is beloved, and the natural world is a constant testament to that love. As a result of the story he tells himself, he survives what others cannot.

I want to tell my story like Piranesi.

Learning to tell a good story is one of the things in life I want to be good at. I've been trying for a while now, and this is what I've learned.

First, I've learned to be aware that I *am* telling a story about life, and to be conscious that it might not be true. We are such good storytellers, you and I, that we come to believe our own stories, and then we obediently play the parts in which we cast ourselves. If you find yourself living the same story over and over again, begin to ask yourself, *Is this story really the inevitable outcome I imagine it to be, or have I told this story to myself so many times that I'm acting it out instinctively, making it true so that at least my life makes sense? Do people really forget and reject me? Or have I practiced that story so many times that I see every action as evidence of their indifference?* Second, I try to tell myself a good story. I don't mean that I try to tell a story in which nothing bad happens; I mean that I try to see myself as a character who meets life difficulties with bravery, cleverness, and perseverance. Life requires different genres for different seasons. Sometimes, I'm Anne of Green Gables, the plucky heroine, greeting each challenge with a candid awkwardness, an eye keen for life's generous beauty, mounting up over personal embarrassments, and fumbling her way into romance. Sometimes I'm Harriet Vane, the cynical writer working her way into tenderness and vulnerability while absolutely killing it professionally. Sometimes I'm Aragorn, carrying a noble sorrow, willing myself each morning not to be consumed by the losses of my own life, but to pour out my life for the healing of others.

Stories still feel like oxygen to me.

I don't often have asthma attacks like I did when I was little, but I still have moments when life makes it hard to breathe, when my chest feels heavy, and desperation makes my head swim and my eyes grow weary. Having stories in my heart that help me imagine how I might face the frustrations, heartbreaks, and challenges of my life is like the quick relief of an inhaler. When it feels impossible to tell a good story, I look to my bookshelves, my Bible, to the saints, to the people in my life who have lived a good story despite all that life could throw their way or take away from them.

But there is another relief too: knowing that I am not the only teller of my story. I remember that before I told my own story, my story was told to me, just like the stories I tell Lilian. Telling ourselves stories is important, but sometimes we lose the thread. We need someone who loves us to wrap us up in their arms and tell us the good story in which we belong. There is a passage from the book *Run with the Horses* by Eugene Peterson, which I hold on to when I'm finding it difficult to tell my own story:

> We enter a world we didn't create. We grow into a life already provided for us. We arrive in a complex of relationships with other wills and destinies that are already in full operation before we are introduced. If we are going to live appropriately, we must be aware that *we are living in the middle of a story that was begun and will be concluded by another.*[1]

As Sarah pointed to the beloved face of Gwennie and said, "She's one of our people," she was introducing Lilian to the "other wills and destinies" that shaped the narrative world in which she lives. But as she grows, she will also learn the larger story—the story that, as Christians, we believe to be most fundamentally true about our lives, whether they end in cancer, or martyrdom, or at an old age surrounded by the people we love. We are wrapped up in the story of a God who is making all things new. When my story feels disjointed, when I lose my voice and I cannot tell it, I fall back into the story that God tells about me.

The Truest Story

I hope someone held you in their lap and told you true stories, but just in case they didn't, I want to tell you the truest story about you.

Once upon a time, the God who fashioned galaxies and mountains and daffodils made you, stitching you together with care and delight. He didn't make you because He needed you, but simply because He is love and love makes beautiful things. He made you like Him, to love and to choose and to make beautiful things.

God knew you wouldn't be perfect, at least not yet, but before you sinned, succeeded, failed, were interesting or boring or beautiful, God treasured you, thought about you, wished good things for you. God has your name written on the palm of His hands. God never forgets you. God is always thinking about how He can help, redeem, restore you. God will never let hurt, anger, abuse, sin, brokenness have the final word in your story.

> I want to tell you the truest story about you.

God loves you so much that He entered into this world of broken stories. He let His head be bowed in grief, He bore the weight of sins He didn't commit, He swallowed up death in His endless self, so that death and sin and pain could never have the final word. With His life, death, and resurrection, He has begun to tell a new story about the world. You enter into that story in baptism; you become a little Christ, dying and rising again, bringing the world itself into the good story of Jesus.

You are God's piece of art, His beautiful poem (Ephesians 2:10). Every day, when you learn to walk in righteousness and truth, the masterpiece that is you is brought closer and closer to completion (Philippians 1:6). God is so proud of each stride that you make; He is not surprised when you stumble. He has given you His Spirit to remind you of His love for you, to empower you to live a brave life. God is with you always, even to the end of the world (Matthew 28:20).

And at that end of all things, God will wipe every tear from your eyes and mine (Revelation 21:4), and He will say to you, "Well done, good and faithful servant!" (Matthew 25:23). We will feast together at the King's beautiful table, and be drawn into the eternal, ever new love of God.

What a good story.

To Read

"On Fairy Stories" by J. R. R. Tolkien

To See

Stranger than Fiction (2006) starring Will Ferrell and
  Emma Thompson

To Listen

"On the Radio" by Regina Spektor

To Ponder

These works of art are about the essential power of story
to shape our lives and choices. What story do you tell yourself? What is the narrator like? What genre is your life story?
Who are the main characters? Who tells your story? Try out
different genres of stories for yourself in a journal. How
might you live differently if you told your story differently?

6

Be like Mr. Collins

You mustn't wish for another life. You mustn't want to be some-
body else. What you must do is this: "Rejoice evermore. Pray without ceasing. In every thing give thanks." I am not all the way capable
of so much, but those are the right instructions.

—Wendell Berry, *Hannah Coulter*

I have long been of the opinion that Mr. Collins of Jane Austen's classic novel *Pride and Prejudice* gets a lot more flack
than he deserves.

Yet another in Jane Austen's long line of odious Anglican
priests (what did they ever do to you, Jane?), Mr. Collins is
one of the most universally derided characters in all of literature or film, whose very name elicits knowing eye rolls and
involuntary huffs of annoyance. Why do people hate him so
much? I suppose one of the main reasons is that he's just *so
annoying*. He says the wrong thing, he doesn't know how to
act at a ball, he proposes to women for whom said proposals

are clearly undesired. Ironically, of course, much of this could be said of Mr. Darcy. The difference here seems to be that Mr. Darcy is handsome and rich, so his lack of tact is *mysterious* and *interesting*, whereas Mr. Collins' is *annoying* and *selfish*. In Mr. Collins' favor, I would argue that at least he tries! His compliments concerning boiled potatoes may be premeditated, but is that not a better approach than sullen silence? (I'm looking at you, Fitzwilliam!).

The greatest mark on Mr. Collins' record, of course, is his skin-crawlingly awkward proposal to Elizabeth Bennet. After laying out some very rational reasons for wishing to marry Miss Elizabeth (that it would greatly add to his happiness! that a good pastor should set an example of matrimony for his parish! that it would keep Elizabeth's childhood home in the family!), he experiences the inconceivable: rejection! Struggling to make sense of this, he attributes this rejection of advances to the "true delicacy of the female character."

No means no, Mr. Collins! Read the room!

Of course, the whole point of Mr. Collins is that he *can't* read the room. That is why we love to hate him. Both in the story and outside of it, Mr. Collins is eminently mockable because we know he doesn't understand that he's being made fun of. But for all his flaws, there is a simplicity to Mr. Collins that I admire and enjoy. He lives in a small and imperturbable world where all that matters is Fordyce's sermons, the securement of a wife for the increase of his happiness, and the distinguished patronage of Lady Catherine de Bourgh. And while we're all laughing at him, Mr. Collins lives in a state of domestic felicity, blessed with a stable life, a meaningful job, and excellent in-laws, satisfied with the choices he has made in life.

Who's laughing now?

Mr. Collins possesses a secret that evades many of the characters in *Pride and Prejudice*, and so often evades me: contentment.

When I think of Mr. Collins, I think of someone who is entirely satisfied with how his life has turned out. This is something I admire. Contentment is a tricky thing because it is easy to either make ourselves miserable wishing we had what other people have, or to settle for too little in life. In this regard, Mr. Collins has something to teach us: he is possessed of a certain kind of humble wisdom, an artfulness at crafting a respectable and satisfactory life, both in the tenacity with which he pursues certain goals, and the humility that enables him to enjoy them fully.

> Contentment is a tricky thing because it is easy to either make ourselves miserable wishing we had what other people have, or to settle for too little in life.

What makes him so contented? I have given this too much thought and I think it boils down (like potatoes) to three things: enjoyment of little things, good ambitions, and a humble acceptance of losses. These are skills essential to the aggressively happy life. Therefore, I propose that we consider how we might emulate the honorable clergyman.

Enjoyment of Little Things

Once, at the end of a catered event I had planned, I found one lonely mini scone left on the serving platter, overflowing with deliciously congealed Devonshire cream and black currant jam.

Scones usually ran out early in the day while the mountain of sandwiches stood resolute and neglected, so, exulting in my good luck, I wrapped it up in foil, and, not having my backpack on hand, stored it in the capacious pocket of my wool coat. Distracted by the flurry of clean-up activities, I forgot about the tiny scone in the completion of my duties.

The next morning, I blearily awoke, dressed, and made coffee before skittering out the door to teach my 9:00 a.m. tutorial. A full day lay ahead of me—teaching, a seminar, two meetings. I ran over the schedule in my mind and wondered if pouring coffee directly into my eyeballs would make me feel more awake. Spotting a motley gaggle of students mulling around the classroom door, I willed myself to look Alert, Older than them, Intelligent, and Professional. I lobbed open the heavy door as the students poured in, depositing themselves around the large rectangular table. Having unceremoniously wiped the whiteboard clean with my be-coated forearm, I reached into my coat pocket in search of the dry erase marker I stored there. (I have a Mary-Poppins-bag arrangement with my coat pockets.)

That was when I felt it: the tiny scone.

I had forgotten all about it! Suddenly, I was awake. A thrill of delight shot through my veins, a more effective stimulant than an IV of coffee. In a flicker of a moment, it occurred to me that I could eat the scone after class. This was a wonderful thought indeed. Maybe I'd steal away between the seminar and the second meeting? Plans formed in my mind to consume it with coffee. Would I have an Americano or a flat white? Definitely an Americano. Black or with milk? It would depend on my mood. And anyway, I had to teach first! *Teaching! Right! I should do that,* I thought. But, oh! This changed everything.

I couldn't suppress a conspiratorial grin. Gathering myself to face the class, I couldn't imagine how they could look so grim on such an auspicious morning as this.

"Good morning, all! Let's dive into this week's reading: what do you make of Augustine's theory of sin as privation?" The rest of the day, there was a bounce in my step and a twinkle in my eye. This little delight illuminated all the banal duties of the day and cast a thrilling sense of secrecy over every conversation. I wondered if people could tell there was something up with me, something special, something secret. People say you should enjoy the little things in life, but that day I was enjoying the mere thought of enjoying the little thing in my pocket, and that secret joy was a sustaining source of levity keeping me afloat.

Learning to take delight in the little things is one of the secrets to an aggressively happy life because it creates an endless source of private delight, and Mr. Collins is an absolute virtuoso at this.

The BBC miniseries perfectly captures Mr. Collins' delight in the little things. Lizzy goes to visit Charlotte and Mr. Collins, and upon her arrival, Mr. Collins shows Lizzy all around his newly spruced-up home in a fever of excitement, as Charlotte graciously refrains from any sign of embarrassment at his overexuberance. While one can't help but feel that Mr. Collins wishes to make Lizzy realize all she's missing out on (a relatable sentiment to anyone who has been romantically rebuffed), it is clear that Mr. Collins' primary motivation is sheer elation at how his life is shaping up. After an extensive tour of the gardens, they arrive in the guest room, where Mr. Collins reveals the pinnacle of his satisfaction with life: shelves in the closet.

"Observe that closet, Cousin Elizabeth. What do you say to that?" says Mr. Collins, almost panting with excitement. Then, unable to wait for a reply from the incredulous Lizzy, he goes on, "Is it not the very essence of practicality and elegance?"

Lizzy smirks, with a teasing condescension she knows Mr. Collins won't perceive, coolly replying with suppressed laughter, "Shelves in the closet. Happy thought indeed!"[1]

Smirk all you want, Cousin Elizabeth. Have you literally ever been as excited about anything as this man is about shelves in a closet?

Really, enjoying the little things is a practice in the art of thankfulness—being conscious of the gifts and good things in your life. Thankfulness is not just something you feel; it's something you practice, which, in turn, shapes the way you think and feel about life. Over and over again in Scripture, we are reminded and shown how to practice thankfulness. "I will give thanks," prays the psalmist (7:17), presumably as a reminder because he doesn't do it naturally. "Give thanks in all circumstances; for this is God's will for you in Christ Jesus," writes Paul to the Thessalonians (1 Thessalonians 5:18). Thankfulness should be our natural posture toward the world, receiving it as a delightful, undeserved gift. Thankfulness is the habit of a heart that notices.

> Enjoying the little things is a practice in the art of thankfulness; being conscious of the gifts and good things in your life.

Let there be no doubt: Mr. Collins has a lucky life, and many things to be thankful for. Not everyone is so fortunate as to secure the venerable patronage of a person like Lady Catherine de Bourgh, or to inherit such a fine estate as Longbourn. The lines have certainly fallen to him in pleasant places, but I do not think that it is mere good fortune that makes Mr. Collins so pleased with his lot in life. Even the most pleasing of worldly ease is not necessarily a guarantee of satisfaction. We see this clearly in the case of another character who shares almost identical circumstances, and yet manages to make himself and many other people deeply unhappy: Mr. Wickham.

Like Mr. Collins, Mr. Wickham is offered a job as a clergyman on the estate at Pemberley, with the younger Mr. Darcy as his patron in almost the exact same arrangement as Mr. Collins. Mr. Wickham even has the better luck of having his education paid for. However, instead of reveling in his good fortune, seeking a ruby of a wife, and trying to be the best vicar he can, Mr. Wickham sets out to reenact the parable of the prodigal son, squandering his wealth on women and drink, and refusing to be useful, studious, or grateful. Unlike the prodigal son, however, there is no repentance in Mr. Wickham, and he lives out his sullen life making problems and manipulating money out of good people.

My point here is that circumstances can certainly aid us in happiness, but they cannot create it. Mr. Collins is a lucky fellow, but he also has the constitution to enjoy it. Through either personality or practice, he has developed a habit of regarding life in a way that enables him to enjoy it. He gives himself fully to the enjoyment of little things and derives a lot of happiness from simple joys. He makes it a point to notice the things in his life about which he is pleased. And there is no joy too small to celebrate. Be it boiled potatoes, the windowpanes at Rosings, or the momentous advent of shelves in a closet, Mr. Collins gives himself over to delight. To put it simply: he has cultivated thankfulness.

In one conversation with Mr. Darcy, Lizzy observes of Lady Catherine, "I am sure she could not have bestowed her kindness on a more grateful object."

And surely, she could not!

The world is teeming with small sources of delight, which often simply go unnoticed. The happy souls who learn to attune their attention to life's miniature generosities obtain for themselves a secret readiness to rejoice in any circumstance. When you really lean in to the pleasure of a strong, sweet cup of tea, or give yourself over to the patient delight of watching raindrops slide down a window, or truly revel in wearing a new blouse that fits and feels just right, each seems like it would be pleasure enough to last a year. When you discipline your attention to both notice and enjoy the little things in life, avenues of delight you could never have imagined open up. How could you be so lucky? Imagine you lived exactly the same life as you do now, but you took the time to notice, cultivate, and enjoy the little pleasures available to you. Wouldn't you be happier?

See, Mr. Collins knows what he's about.

Good Ambitions

Can I confess something to you?

When I took the Pottermore quiz to see which Hogwarts house I belonged to, I came out a Slytherin. To those for whom this means nothing, let me explain. The houses are sorted according to the values each house holds and the predominant character qualities each student possesses. Gryffindor values bravery, Hufflepuff hard work, and Ravenclaw intelligence. Slytherin, however, is the "bad guys" house, and their value is almost a vice: ambition. All my friends objected that it must have been a mistake, I must have messed something up on the test. "You're a Gryffindor!" they cooed.

But in my heart, I knew it was true: I am a Slytherin.

My mother likes to tell a story from when I was a very little girl (three, I think). We were at a county fair, and she momentarily lost track of me. After a moment of glancing around in panic, she spotted me. I was very determinedly elbowing my way through a packed crowd of oblivious children and adults. The story goes that I confidently parted a Red Sea of older, larger people, planted myself before a pen of baby goats, and watched the baby goats intently until I'd had my fill, at which point I calmly elbowed my way back through the crowd, satisfied in having achieved my goal.

I have always had a motor running inside of me, a sense of all the things I could accomplish or create, all the people I could lead. I'm told that I often complained to my mother that she wasn't "doing enough with me" academically. (In hindsight, this is extremely comical given the fact I started my PhD studies at age twenty-two). I often remind myself of my family's dog, Darcy (not Fitzwilliam of Pemberley). A large portion of caring for this sweet and ridiculous creature is keeping her from injuring herself in pursuit of tennis balls. Since she was twelve weeks old, she has had a monomaniacal interest in playing fetch. On numerous occasions, she has injured herself in pursuit of a ball, either by hitting her paw on a sprinkler head, or writhing too enthusiastically to snatch the ball from the air, or running too fast. Her devotion to the art of fetch is to be commended, but there's a certain tragedy to it; can her love of catching balls be fulfilled without injury to herself? Can my ambition run free without exhausting me?

The Cambridge dictionary provides two main definitions of ambition: "strong desire for success, achievement, power, or wealth" or "a strong wish to achieve something."[2] One emphasizes the activity of ambition, and the other the object of ambition, and in this distinction there exists a world of difference. To desire to achieve something is not wrong; indeed, shouldn't we all strongly wish to achieve things? A virtuous life? Meaningful relationships? Financial stability? Eternal life? The problem is not ambition, but the goal of our ambitions.

One of the insidious tricks modern society has played upon us is that it values ambition as an activity but fails to furnish us with worthwhile objects of our ambition. The modern world preys on people like me because, like Darcy, we'll work ourselves into injury and not ask why. We have an impoverished vision of a meaningful life, so we encourage people toward an insatiable pursuit of goods that do them no good without a community, a moral framework within which to enjoy them. When we hallow ambition itself as a good, we make way for lives on a treadmill, eternally running but getting nowhere. This is the culture that gobbles up all the resources of the earth and economy and still isn't full. As Colin Firth wryly observes in *Mamma Mia: Here We Go Again*: "There's no use climbing the ladder if you're on completely the wrong wall. "[3]

So what do we do? Do we give up on ambition altogether? Darcy strained her paw again recently, and as she mopes around the house, searching for a tennis ball she will not find (because we have hidden them all), I wonder: is there a healthy outlet for all this energy in *me*? Am I bound to be dissatisfied with life? To wound my metaphorical paw?

Mr. Collins is certainly a Slytherin, but he has no such anxieties.

He has ambition, yes. We know from the very first page where we meet Mr. Collins that he desires to achieve certain things in life, but his ambitions in life are few, simple, and achievable. He has no malice toward anyone. He does not wish to trample anyone under his feet on the road to worldly success, and that is more than can be said of most Austen characters. He's very determined in his pursuit of a good wife, but his main ambition, it seems, is to live a respectable, dutiful, and comfortable life. He is neither passive in his pursuit of these goals nor possessed of the insatiable hunger for more. He makes it his ambition to live a good and happy life, and to do his duty by the people around him. And when he achieves these goals, he is well satisfied. We never see any sign that he is tortured by something that someone else has. He is not a jealous man. If a bishopric were to come his way, well, I'm sure he'd be overjoyed at his good luck, and he'd do his very best. It might even go to his head a bit, but I think he'd do his duty with the same solemnity and satisfaction with which he tamed his garden.

When he finally marries Charlotte (the only honest character in the entire story), Mr. Collins is quite literally as happy as he can be. He works in his garden. He delights in his beehives. His great joy each week is to dine at Rosings Park with the auspicious Lady Catherine de Bourgh. He can't believe his luck to have been stationed as the parish priest at Rosings, and he wants to do a very good job by his patron. He is entirely pleased with his choice of wife, and to Charlotte's great satisfaction, he keeps himself busy, so she can enjoy a room all to herself, where he is not to bother her. He has made a good life for himself, a steady, beautiful life, which others can depend on and he can enjoy. And enjoy it he does!

Mr. Collins seems to have taken the apostle Paul's command seriously:

> Make it your ambition to lead a quiet life: You should mind your own business and work with your hands, just as we told you, so that your daily life may win the respect of outsiders and so that you will not be dependent on anybody.
>
> 1 Thessalonians 4:11–12

I love this verse because it doesn't tell us to destroy ambition, but to give it a worthy and achievable aim. The goal described is not a stockpile of resources (wealth, fame, status), but the attainment of a way of being in the world: a "quiet life." So much is contained in the brief description this verse gives. A life that is peaceful, not flashy, humble, tranquil. A life with meaningful work to do ("work with your hands"), whose fruits you can observe in tangible ways. A life that will "win the respect of outsiders," a life of congruity and integrity, respectable and worthy of admiration. A life that is reliable, self-sustaining ("you will not be dependent on anybody"), a source of stability to others, and a calm in the storm of life.

Such is the life that Mr. Collins has achieved. Such is the life that I desire.

To live a quiet life of contentment, where your goal is stability and not eternal accumulation, is a radical thing in this insatiable world of ours. When your aim is a quiet life, ambition becomes the friend of contentment and not the foe. If greater achievements come your way, relish them, but do not tie your happiness to that star. I cannot help but think what a gentler and more life-giving world it would be if we bent our ambition toward the goal of a quiet life. We would be less lonely, because we would have valued family, community, and home more than the endless ascent of a career ladder that leads nowhere. Our world would groan less under the weight of unfettered and irresponsible consumption, because we would value sustainability and self-sufficiency. We would feel less restless, because we would be satisfied that our quiet life was good, and enough.

> **I cannot help but think what a gentler and more life-giving world it would be if we bent our ambition toward the goal of a quiet life.**

We'd be happier, because we'd have the satisfaction of achieving a life that provides sustenance to ourselves and others, which adds and does not detract from the stability of the world.

Just like Mr. Collins.

Humble Acceptance of Losses

People like to say that the test of a person's character is not failure but success, but I think this assumes we all succeed a lot more than we actually do. In my experience, failure, rejection, or loss is the much more common and continual test of character in one's life than success. No matter how clever, or thankful, or well-meaning we are, life simply will not always go our way; someone else will get the job, the girl, the accolade. Much of our happiness will depend on how we handle these losses. Whether we choose to become bitter, or to blame ourselves, or to vow not to put ourselves out there again, or to be satisfied with what we have been given, how we handle loss shapes how we face the future and how we feel about life. The closest I come to despising Mr. Collins and feeling he truly has shown a vice is after his sloppy and conceited proposal, followed by his astonished refusal to believe that Elizabeth could possibly say no to such a fine catch as himself. (You have to respect the self-confidence.) Now, before we indulge in a Mr. Collins hate-fest, you must remember that in his mind, he was doing right by his cousins. Because he stood to inherit the estate, finding a wife amongst the Bennets would have ensured that none of Lizzy's four siblings or mother would have to be turned out upon Mr. Bennet's death. So, he simply surveyed the sisters and picked the best one. He was not unreasonable to think this might be a good idea, and it is not a crime to be socially awkward.

But, of course, Elizabeth was right to refuse him. She did not love him, and, rightly or not, she did not respect him. Life is more than an economic calculus.

But still, Mr. Collins balks. Mr. Collins is simply encountering the uncomfortable reality that every person you date will either marry or break up with you. I suppose in the Regency era, this could be applied to proposals since they seem to skip the courtship, for the most part. The whole endeavor of romance opens us up to the alarming possibility that our happiness could depend on someone else, and other people have minds, wills, and desires that might be entirely dissonant with our own! The horror!

And this speaks to the even larger reality that no matter how kind you are, not everyone in the world will like you. At some point or another, we all encounter rejection. I have been on the receiving end of my fair share of rejection in many areas of life and have also been the one doing the rejection. Both give you an interesting perspective on the manifold ways in which we attempt to protect ourselves and shield our embarrassment, either by becoming vindictive and haughty, or indulging in self-hatred and moping. It seems that it is very difficult to simply say, "Well, that's a bummer. I wish it had turned out a different way. But I wish you well!"

How can we achieve this?

When I was a little girl, my mother made me and my siblings memorize the classic British poem "If" by Rudyard Kipling, which describes an ideal of British manhood. One stanza always particularly stood out to me:

> If you can make one heap of all your winnings
> And risk it on one turn of pitch-and-toss,
> And lose, and start again at your beginnings
> And never breathe a word about your loss.[4]

Feeling that it is obvious that this book is not pro-suppressing-your-feelings-and-becoming-a-robot, I wish to make the following point: there is a virtue in learning to suck it up, take it on the chin, and carry on with your life. Denying the urge to give in to indulgent self-pity or vindictive character assassination of whoever has rejected you (be it a boss or boyfriend) will actually make you feel and look better in the end. I sometimes feel that in the world of spilling all our guts online, we have lost the art of personal dignity. In my life, I have found it is almost always better to (at least publicly) accept rejection without "breathing a word about your loss."

How do we find it in ourselves to do this? Well, I think first of all, we must have a sense of our own value and dignity. Dignified country vicars do not beg for someone to change their minds! And they certainly do not mope! When you experience rejection, try to manage the feeling of rising panic. Take a deep breath. Preserve your dignity. If you have a hard time imagining how you should do this, just imagine yourself to be any one of Maggie Smith's characters in any movie, and act like that. Would the Dowager Countess cry if someone said something mean to her? No! How vulgar! Would Professor McGonagall mope around Hogwarts and insist all her friends make her feel better about herself if someone defied her? Preposterous!

There is a virtue in learning to suck it up, take it on the chin, and carry on with your life.

But of course, merely preserving your dignity is not enough, because this attitude can harden into a cynical outlook on life in which you are never willing to put yourself out there either in romance, work, or friendship, and that is no recipe for happiness. After the first sting of rejection, and a dignified public acceptance of defeat, you must learn to privately accept rejection in a way that feeds neither bitterness nor helplessness.

Practicing thankfulness prior to rejection helps soften the blow because you are already aware of how abundant your life is. It is when we cease being thankful for our own lives and begin to envy others that we make ourselves most miserable. I often think of Peter at the very end of Jesus' earthly ministry. After Jesus tells him about his future suffering, his response is to ask about John's fate. Jesus responds, "What is that to you? You must follow me" (John 21:22). God does not owe us an easy life; our crushes do not owe us a returned affection. We cannot live our lives demanding that we be given exactly what everyone else has. When we find ourselves seething with jealousy, we must remember Jesus' words: "What is that to you, Joy? *You* follow me."

Each of us has our own story to tell, our own life to live. That life will have losses, real things to be sad and bummed about. But comparison only adds to that frustration. Pay attention to your own puzzle, and do not let bitterness take its root. When I stop demanding that life be a certain way and attend instead to the generous confines of my own life, I find I am able to accept rejection. I can say to myself *I didn't win that one, but it's okay. Look at all the good things in my life. I am a very lucky person.*

But just because you aren't owed anything in life doesn't mean you shouldn't try for some things. Think, again, dear reader, of Mr. Collins. If he had accepted total defeat and crawled into a hole of eternal bachelorhood, he would never have won the treasure of Charlotte, dear Charlotte. I really dislike how the 2005 film adaptation of *Pride and Prejudice* portrays Charlotte as some haggard and desperate old maid of twenty-seven who scrapes by in life by marrying an annoying priest. Tosh! Charlotte makes for herself a fine and comfortable life; she has weighed and measured her options, and this is the one she has chosen. And lucky Mr. Collins! Charlotte is even-tempered, a good mistress of the home, and as undramatic as beans on toast! And think of his in-laws. At the end of *Pride and Prejudice*, I always think to myself how awkward family Christmases must be for the Bennet/Darcy/Bingley/Wickham extended household. You could hardly comment on the weather without mentioning a verboten son-in-law or raising the ire of a sarcastic sister-in-law. But Mr. Collins? He dodges all that. His in-laws are the lovely Lucases, fine, undramatic gentle people.

Though Lizzy's initial rejection may have stung, Mr. Collins should count his blessings, for they are plenteous. And you know what's great? I know he will count his blessings!

Perhaps even after all this you will *still* insist that Mr. Collins is laughable, and I would say that there is one more lesson that we have to learn from him: do not care too much of what other people think of you. Do not care even if they think your life is silly. While we all laugh and chortle about how weird he is, Mr. Collins is living his best life now.

Mr. Collins has the last laugh.

To Read

"If" by Rudyard Kipling

To See

The BBC miniseries *Pride and Prejudice* (1995) starring
  Jennifer Ehle and Colin Firth

To Listen

"The Gift" by Jon Foreman

"Don't You Want to Thank Someone" by Andrew Peterson

To Ponder

These artworks are about cultivating thankfulness, endurance, and virtuous ambition.

   What do you want out of life? Write out a list of what your ambition of a quiet and simple life would be like. How might you take one bold step toward that future? Now practice thankfulness; make a list of all the tiny things that bring you joy. What are your metaphorical "shelves in the closet"? What brings you great delight?

7

Believe in God

If we are faithless, He remains faithful, for He cannot deny Himself.

—2 Timothy 2:13 NASB

This again? I thought. *Will I ever be rid of it?*

It had come upon me once more, the great drowsiness of doubt. Believing in God has never been easy for me, and yet it has always felt important. To the consternation of both my believing and unbelieving friends, I continually found myself washed away in a tide of questions, with a panicky desire to land on the shores of belief. I was so, so tired of it. I wanted to believe in God, but then questions that I had resigned to mystery seemed urgent and impossible again. That day, the muscle of belief within me slackened, limped, and snapped. From the fragile bravery of faith I had fought so hard to maintain, I drew back. Someone I had begun to love, you see, had died. In a town far away, he had slipped away on a spring morning, with no warning and no good-bye. And, somehow, I had known it would happen—and I hated that I knew.

Since living in St. Andrews, the sea had become my confidant. The din of the shore affords a kind of privacy. I often sang, recited poetry, or spoke aloud while I walked, my words and tunes safely hidden in the babble of rushing water, the ironical cackling of seagulls, the ferocity of an easterly wind. The ocean keeps her secrets, and I loved her for it. That day, I walked on the seashore, letting the crash of waves muffle the undignified moans of my broken heart, bearing out my grief with the receding tide. When the first rush of tears was spent, I wiped my face and ordered a meal over the phone to send to the grieving family in the faraway town. It was the one thing I could do, the one way I could help in what seemed like a helpless situation. I plodded back to my flat with angry, heavy steps, talking to God, but not listening.

> **I wanted to believe in God, but then questions, which I resigned to mystery, seemed urgent and impossible again.**

People die every day.

People that you say you love.

How can you say you love them?

Why do you let this happen over and over again?

Some friend you are, God!

If you're real, why do you make it so hard to believe in you?

In that moment, the prospect of God's existence seemed more offensive to me than His absence. His existence gnawed at me. If God didn't exist, there was nothing to be angry about— the world was frightening and random, but not malicious. But if God did exist, and He allowed this ugliness, this pain, this injustice to go on and on, generation after generation . . . how could it be borne? My grief wrapped itself in a mantle of seething rage, my helplessness in indignation. It is easier, I have realized, to feel angry than to feel afraid or sad. Anger is bold and assertive, makes its demands, expects something. In anger, I could stave off the devastation lurking beneath the incurable ache and confusion of loss, and the fear that maybe this, at last, was too much. That this time, I could no longer hold on to faith.

I felt lost and loss, but I raged because it made me feel safer.

I refused to listen to God because I was afraid He wouldn't speak.

And a month passed.

Spring break came, and along with it a friend from America. I did my best to tuck my Pandora's questions back into their box. At the very least, I turned my eyes away from them. They hissed and sputtered and threatened at every moment to spread like lava over everything, but I did my best to ignore them. Jessica came, a shock of red curly hair and boundless enthusiasm. Her cheerfulness revived me slightly, and it was a relief to be distracted. Many generations past, her family had been natives of the Borderlands in Scotland, the strip of land that, throughout history, was sometimes England and sometimes Scotland, depending on who had most recently killed whom. When her great-, great-, great-, great-, great-grandfather had lived there, it was a violent, uncertain place. People in power threw military punches back and forth, trying to grab swaths of land, and the country people were always caught in between. Opportunistic men took advantage of the instability, pillaging family farms when armies did not. So Jessica's family did what had to be done and built a guard tower, keen eyed and impenetrable. Her old relative watched deep into the dark night for signs of intruders and mischief makers in order to keep the people of the valley safe.

The tower still exists, and, in a pleasant turn of fate, is now a vacation rental property. So we set out to the land of Jessica's ancestors to stay in a seventeenth-century tower. As one does.

After a bumpy hour and a half in a double-decker bus that careened its way down country roads, we disembarked in a tiny town and sought groceries. Weighed down with eggs, tea, toast, mushrooms, and plentiful rashers of bacon for the next morning's feast, we found a map and began our trek. The first two hours were beautiful. We walked along a sparkling stream, we passed a once grand castle, its crumbling stones seemingly frozen in their rumble down the hill. At one point, the path led to the mouth of an abandoned railway tunnel cheerfully spray painted by the local youth. Farther on, we passed through a large field whose only occupant was an imperturbable pheasant. We hadn't spent much time together since high school, so there was a great deal to catch up on. We talked in easy, laughing rhythm, remembering our earnest and embarrassing youthful dreams, recounting the triumphs, insights, and defeats of the foregoing year, playfully imagining what our futures might hold. So easy was this conversation that we hardly noticed it had begun to get dark.

We became slightly worried. Surely, we thought, we must have walked too far. We noticed a road that wrapped around a field; the map didn't seem to have a road. This was concerning. The groceries and our backpacks began to feel very heavy. There had been no sign of civilization for a good thirty minutes.

We fruitlessly gazed at our map, turning it upside down, trying to discern some landmark, hoping it might reveal some secret mystery. The pheasant stared on indifferently as we began to make contingency plans. It was then that our savior appeared. She was wearing Wellington boots, carrying a ball thrower, and had a jaunty black Lab at her side. She smiled, her cherry cheeks aglow with the exercise and cool air, her pleasantly wrinkled eyes sparkling with friendliness.

"You two look lost!" she said, with a gentle Scottish trill.

"We're trying to find the Barnett Tower. We're staying there tonight."

"The Tower! Well, of course. I know the place. My daughter is staying there for her honeymoon in a few months' time. Lovely place."

"Oh wonderful!" we said in unison relief. "Where is it?"

"Just a mile downstream!"

Our faces must have fallen, because the kind lady immediately offered to drive us. We gratefully agreed, and, forgetting everything our parents had ever said about not getting in the car of a stranger, we walked around the field and piled into her country SUV, which smelled of car freshener and dog food. The Lab, confined to the trunk, leaned its head over our seats and dolefully drooled on my shoulder, while our generous chauffeur happily chattered away in melodic brogue, pointing out this sixteenth-century bridge over here and old Angus's farm over there. After a few minutes we rounded the corner and found ourselves in the shadow of Barnett Tower.

I don't know what I had expected to see, but somehow I didn't expect an actual, honest-to-goodness tower. But there it was: a thirty-foot tall, twelve-foot square stalwart pillar of stone.

The wind whistled around it, a small bush splayed against its unforgiving base in the merciless gust. It was properly dark and cold by this time, so after effusively thanking our benefactress, Jessica wasted no time searching under the appropriate (empty) flowerpot for a cartoonishly large skeleton key. I wouldn't exactly call Barnett Tower inviting, but its wooden door with a skeleton lock gaping like an open mouth did stir the kind of curiosity in me that caves, crawl spaces, and attics did in my childhood. As we scurried over the well-trodden threshold, I couldn't help but feel I was entering the fairy queen's palace, never to emerge.

In a happy contradiction, the interior of the tower was as cozy as the exterior was foreboding. Each of its four floors was composed of a single, spacious room with sagging ceilings: the bottom floor a mudroom, the second floor a well-equipped kitchen with cheerful dishware and a gas stove, the third floor a comfortable living room with bookshelves heavy laden with crime novels and Scottish tourism guides, and the top floor a bedroom with a vast king-sized bed modestly clothed in a homemade quilt and a snug woolen throw. Having shed our groceries on the kitchen floor and lugged our backpacks all the way up four flights of ladders, we let our baggage tumble to the ground and threw ourselves on the spacious bed, laughing at our adventure and our good fortune of being ferried there by a native. We practically had a whole castle to ourselves, and the delight of it was not lost on us.

Drawn by the audible grumblings of our stomachs, we set out to make dinner, which was some combination of toast, cheese, bacon, and giant mugs of tea. Our phone speakers strained at max volume to aid our merry dance of cooking and singing and laughing. The buoyancy of Jessica's hair and spirits pulled my own dour disposition into a happy rhythm. We laughed and ate and watched an old-fashioned, feel-good movie. I almost forgot I was having a spiritual crisis. Wearied by the long wander, we gratefully crawled into bed and fell without hesitation into a deep, satisfying slumber.

In the early hours of the morning, the wind's relentless moaning woke me, and a deep sadness settled over my soul. I lay on my back, staring at the blackness above me, which I presumed to be ceiling, hoping sleep would graciously deign to visit me again. It did not. Resigning myself, I slipped out of bed and carefully descended the ladder. I made a cup of tea, pressed *shuffle* on a playlist on my iPhone, wrapped myself in a woolen throw, and perched by the one small window in the kitchen. It hadn't struck me till that moment how few windows there were in the tower. *But of course*, I thought, *this was a watchtower, a place of military defense. Windows were a liability.* And as the wind rattled the window with petulant urgency, I thought perhaps they still were.

I think it was something about the safety of the tower, but as I sat there, with the mug radiating its heat into my morning-chilled fingers, my cloak of anger fell off, and beneath it I found a great sadness, a great fear, and a great weariness.

Here was the sadness: loss cannot be cured. One of my friends says the people we love are like suns around whom we orbit, and when we lose someone, one of our most profound feelings is that of a loss of gravity. We no longer know up from down, we are sent spinning into space, wondering what there is to hold on to. But life is full of these perishable suns—it cannot be helped. We are born into a world where suns can be counted, tossed from year to weary year with mutable solar systems.

I knew this, and in many moments past I had reconciled myself to it. It seemed to me that God exists, that He loves us, and that the world is full of pain and bent toward death. Long ago, I had come to think that these things could, mysteriously, be true at the same time, and that I would rather live with God in pain than turn my back on God because this world of His doesn't make sense. Why, then, this sudden recapitulation of doubt? Why this renewed paralysis of faith?

I suppose because sometimes, no matter how intellectual, or spiritual, or mature we are, the brokenness of the world is too hard to bear, and the eyes of faith are blurred by tears. I had confessed, with Paul, Christ resurrected—a confession for which, if wrong, I was of all women to be pitied. Again and again, I had stumbled, fallen, and clung to the rock of Christ, feeling Him to be the truest thing, and the best, the most real. In moments I had felt this truth as clear and close as my heartbeat. But in my grief, it all seemed suddenly untrue, a desperate grasping for permanence in the chasm of impermanence. The mirage of water seen by a man dying of thirst in the desert. I felt myself to be pathetic, and God apathetic.

Here was the fear: that I had wasted my time. I had been straining my eyes, my heart, my faith to see the mirage and believe it was true. I felt somewhere in the corners of my heart that if I gave up on God, He would give up on me. I was weary of holding the reasons I still believed in God and His goodness before my eyes, and feeling abandoned by Him. I was worried I'd fought hard to hold on to a faith in a God who wasn't there, or worse, who didn't listen. *I should not*, I thought honestly, *have to try so hard*. I feared my faith would end like T. S. Eliot's "The Hollow Men": "Not with a bang but a whimper."[1]

I would quietly resign myself to agnosticism, and God would do nothing about it.

And perhaps most of all, I was weary. Weary of being here again. Once more unsure, afraid. Worried it would always be like this. Dryly, and with an ache in my throat, I closed my eyes.

God, I want to believe in you. I haven't found anything more beautiful, more true. But I have nothing left. I cannot summon up one more drop of belief. I am dry. I can't see what difference it makes. If you want me to stick around . . .

I felt somewhere in the corners of my heart that if I gave up on God, He would give up on me.

I paused. I don't know what I wanted from God. To say something? Do something? To apologize? Whatever it was, I honestly didn't expect God to live up to the challenge. I thought there would be only silence, that I would resign myself to either belief or agnosticism, with no advice from the heavens.

But then two things happened.

Choosing a Sun to See By

In the incredibly long and cathartically depressing Russian novel *The Brothers Karamazov,* there is a short story that you almost certainly had to read for your high school literature class: "The Grand Inquisitor." It is an elaborate parable where Jesus comes back to earth during the Inquisition and is put to death all over again by people who cannot or refuse to recognize the Savior they claim to worship. The story is a part of a longer conversation between two brothers, Ivan and Alyosha. Ivan is a worldly and academic young man, and Alyosha a postulant who wants to become a monk. In a shadowy corner of a tavern, they argue about how one is to make sense of this shadowed world of ours.

They each adopt youthful postures of atheism and theism, earnest and uncomplicated in their convictions, possessing more fervor than nuance. And yet, in each of them there is an admirable honesty. Ivan looks at the cruelty of humanity, the way we not only fall short of goodness but go to great lengths to hurt each other, and concludes there is not a God, or at least not a loving one. Why would you even want to believe in a God who made a world like this? he asks Alyosha. Even if the whole world were beautiful and good but one child was left alone to suffer in the dark, Ivan thinks God could not be worthy of devotion.

Alyosha is troubled by Ivan's doubts, which live in his own heart too, but he maintains that life is made more sensible, more beautiful when it is lived *as though* God exists. The more one lives inside the story of Christianity, the more undeniable it becomes. He cannot make sense of it all, but he feels it to be true in his bones.

The Brothers Karamazov is not Christian propaganda. It presents both atheism and Christianity in their strongest, most convincing lights, and leaves them dangling in your mind. As you read Ivan's words, you can see clearly that the conclusions he draws are not unreasonable. He has a keen conscience and a good mind, and, with all the sincerity in his heart, he simply cannot believe. Alyosha is full of his own doubts too, but he has chosen to live inside the story of Christ, and it costs him greatly. The story is not a simplistic morality tale where belief is the obvious conclusion, and the life of faith clean and certain. The book explores belief not through argument, but through lived experience. Ivan's relentless rationalism drives him to madness, where Alyosha's faith invites him to a life of forgiveness and love and meaning, even as doubt lingers. The reader cares for both characters and empathizes with their points of view.

I think that Fyodor Dostoevsky was able to convey both the atheism of Ivan and the childlike faith of Alyosha so vividly and sympathetically because both belief and unbelief lived and wrestled inside of him. Alyosha and Ivan were the two sets of eyes through which life taught Dostoevsky to see the world. His childhood was a contradiction of love, faith, and pain. His parents cared for him deeply and showed him a living faith, but like the suffering child in Ivan's story, Dostoevsky suffered frequent seizures and was bewildered by the isolation and pain of this experience. As a young writer, he was arrested and sentenced to execution with his writing circle for being an intellectual radical. The firing squad halted only moments before they were commanded to shoot. He went on to serve four years in a prison camp in Siberia, followed by two years of compulsory military service. The squalor and cruelty he experienced in exile are vividly portrayed in his novels, many of which are viscerally upsetting, unveiling the darkest depravity of human nature.

As he boarded the train to Siberia, a woman gave him a copy of the four gospels, the only book he was allowed to have with him in exile. He became devoted, even obsessed, with the person of Jesus. This little book was a solace to him in his darkest years, but he wrestled deeply to reconcile the deep darkness and suffering he had experienced with the love of God. Upon being released from prison, physically weak and psychologically traumatized, he wrote to the woman who sent the Gospels, saying he was "a child of unbelief and doubt up to this very moment, and I am certain that I shall remain so to the grave."[2] Like Ivan, Dostoevsky was haunted by the specter of all the secret suffering in the world; he was too honest to suppress his doubts, and too sincere to fake being a believer. And yet as haunted as Dostoevsky was by the darkness of the world, he was all the more haunted by Christ. Like Alyosha, he could not get the story of Christianity out of his bones: the God who would bend down to the world, enter into the suffering of the lonely child, receive scars into His divine body. Tutored by the mystery of the stars and galaxies on which he loved to gaze, he came to hold a faith rooted in love and wonder. Like Alyosha, he chose Christ not merely because it was the most logical thing to do, but because life was more vital, more beautiful, more real, more congruent, when he lived as though it was true.

In "The Weight of Glory," C. S. Lewis wrote, "I believe in Christianity as I believe that the Sun has risen, not only because I see it but because by it, I see everything else."[3] Lewis thought there was a difference between looking at something and looking through it. In one of his most poignant essays, he describes standing in a toolshed and seeing a shaft of light pierce the dusty darkness. Looking *at* the sunbeam, you can say various things about it, and describe it. But if you step *into* the sunbeam, if you look *through* it, it will offer you something you could never experience from the outside, staring at it from a distance. Ivan was only willing to look at the sunbeam of faith, but Alyosha wanted to see through it. Perhaps Ivan had good reasons; he was afraid he was only going to be taken in, that it is all an illusion. And perhaps it is. There's always a risk in faith. Anyone who tells you otherwise is probably selling something. But we all have faith in something. Even atheism rests on the faith that God does not exist. It sees life through the shadowed light of unbelief, whether with a wistful fatalism or mortal urgency. Ivan may say to Alyosha, *What if God doesn't exist?* But Alyosha can justly respond, *What if God does?*

Alyosha was willing to stand within the shaft of light, to see by it and through it, to let it suffuse his perception and experience. Even on the days when it all seemed very unlikely, Christianity made more sense of his fractured life. If it was a lie, it was a beautiful lie that called him to lay down his life, to see grace in everything, to believe that nothing is lost forever. It was no mere soporific consolation in the face of death; it was a clarion call to generosity, forgiveness. It did not make everything easier, but it made it meaningful, bearable, vivid. In his old age, Dostoevsky was known to say, "Even if someone were to prove to me that the truth lay outside Christ, I should choose to remain with Christ rather than with the truth."[4] Perhaps this sounds like heresy to some ears, and blind faith to others, but I think he knew something essential. Faith is not merely about affirming the statements that we can quantifiably know are true; it is about walking in the light of a mystery we can't understand but that illuminates the path before us. We can stare into the sun, blinding ourselves in our attempts to comprehend that which can only be apprehended in the flesh-and-bone struggle of life. Or we can always stand outside the beam, too afraid to be fooled. Or we can step into it. Taste. See.

The struggle between faith and despair has been at the heart of my battle for happiness. I once asked my mother if she'd still love me if I was agnostic all my life. She immediately answered, "Of course I would." And as I breathed a sigh of relief, she said, "But I think you'd be happier with God." And she was right. I know that when I stand inside faith, when I see through its rays, I find a beauty, an inner resonance. My life makes more sense; I find in myself something vital and indefatigable. Sometimes, I waver, afraid of being fooled or tired of grieving, but the beam is always there. The question is not if it is there, but if I will choose to see by it, to live by it.

The feelings of belief and unbelief may come and go, but each of us must choose which sun to live by.

The Fragile Wings of Faith

The first thing that happened was that my iPhone began to play "Jesus' Blood Never Failed Me Yet." I actually gasped, and tears sprung immediately to my eyes. Faith fluttered, weary but alive in my chest.

I first heard the Jars of Clay version of this song in college and found it oddly haunting. Years later, I learned that this song was originally arranged by Gavin Bryars in 1971, while he was scoring a soundtrack for a documentary on homelessness in London. While hunting through hundreds of hours of film, he stumbled upon something he found rather remarkable: a homeless man, in his right mind, peaceful, singing a familiar-sounding and yet unidentifiable hymnic tune with this simple chorus:

Jesus' blood never failed me yet, never failed me yet,
  never failed me yet,
This one thing I know, that he loves me so.

Bryars realized that the tune formed a perfect loop, and his composer's curiosity was awakened. He began to layer the track with simple strings, swelling with greater depth in each repetition. He didn't intend to use the composition for the documentary; it just felt important to do. One day, he left the track playing on a loop and went off to make a cup of coffee. When he returned to his cubicle, he was met by an unnatural hush. His officemates were listening to the loop, singing out the doorway of his office. They were somber, struck silent, the eyes of some swimming with tears. Something in this piece of music was true, profound, inexpressible.

I learned this history in a lecture about atonement theories during my master's course. The story came at the end of a lecture in which we explored various theories about how we can understand the death and resurrection of Christ to enable salvation—the ransom theory, that God ransomed us from the devil's power; the satisfaction theory, that Jesus fulfilled the perfect demands of God so we didn't have to; the scapegoat theory, in which Jesus takes away the stain of our sin. The professor pointed out that soteriology (the theology of salvation) has never been a matter of conciliar orthodoxy; while the councils of Nicaea ruled on the natures of Jesus, or the doctrine of the Trinity, no final word has ever been spoken about the nature of salvation. To be a faithful, orthodox Christian, you do not need to explain how Jesus' death saves you; you need only know that it *does.*

"For all our theological debates, all our parsing of words, and all the important distinctions," said our professor, "all that the church asks of us is to make as simple a confession as this man. Not to explain it, but to trust that Jesus' blood does the work we cannot."

And then we sat together as a class, quietly listening to the frail voice surrounded and uplifted by the breathing beauty of strings. The arrangement dignified the simple confession of the old man, gently coming around it, lifting it up, making this confession from the gutter sound like the song of the martyrs in paradise. It struck me that the arrangement was a beautiful embodiment of grace, coming around a rasping confession, honoring it, and making it enough. Isn't this what God does with our faith? He takes the mustard seeds of our sputtering confessions and undergirds them with the melody of His grace, rejoicing in them, lifting them up, making them sufficient.

"Lord, I believe," cried the fearful father to Jesus. "Help my unbelief!" (Mark 9:24 NKJV).

And He did.

In that moment, I realized belief is not something we perform, something we are saved by. This is the gospel: that we are miserable, that we make ourselves miserable, that we cannot save ourselves, but that God loves us, and in His mercy, saves us, asking nothing in return but that we live in the wholeness and union for which we were intended. My doubt made me miserable, and I thought I could save myself through belief. I had made myself miserable, again and again, trying to summon, nurture, maintain a belief sure enough to save me from the hell of my own uncertainty. But this is not faith: it is performance, it is fear, it is certainty. Faith is confessed like a sin thrown upon the mercy of God. And God makes beautiful our confessions. This was the grace I had always experienced in doubt, God making my stuttering confessions enough, asking no more of me than to hum to myself in the gutter of my uncertainty and trust that Jesus' blood truly would not fail me.

162

To my great embarrassment, tears sprung into my eyes. I quietly tried to blink them back, not even raising a hand to stem the tide. The professor looked directly at me. (How did she know?)

"It is beautiful, isn't it?"

And it was.

All of this rushed back to me in the tower. Tears rolled down my cheeks, and a palpable peace washed over me. I laughed at myself. *This? Again?* I thought, *Will I ever learn?* Had I not been back in the old trap of trying to believe hard enough to save myself from suffering, from pain, from unbelief? Jesus had, once again, placed my hands in His wounds and said, "No longer doubt, but believe" (John 20:27). And in that moment, I did. I believed with my whole heart. This was relief, but no assurance. But when would I *get it*? When would I get off the merry-go-round? When would I know, or give up knowing?

Can I doubt after this? I thought to myself wistfully. *Will this be the last time?*

I heard in my heart a response: *Yes, and you will again.*

And I knew I would. I knew there would be other days when the whole thing would seem very unlikely. Days when pain or fear or weariness would cloud my vision. Days when I slipped back into trying to save myself through effort, through performing belief, through proving to God (as though He needed my help) that He exists. There would be days I would forget about God. Days where the whole business seemed like too much effort. For a moment, I saw myself clearly, and I knew how frail and fickle and frenetic I was. And I knew that I did not surprise Jesus one bit. I knew also that it was not my effort that had held me in the faith all these years, like I sometimes liked to think it was. It was grace, a force totally outside of me. Pleading, appealing, upholding. Calling out to me in sermons and sacraments, in sunrises and playlists. I was held though I did not hold. And I always would be.

I knew that it was not my effort that had held me in the faith all these years, like I sometimes liked to think it was. It was grace.

It was then that the second thing happened.

In the periphery of my vision, I sensed a fluttering, a movement of wings. A butterfly landed on the windowsill *inside* the tower. Where had she come from? I was on the second floor, and every window was shut tight. It was not the time for butterflies yet. It was early spring, and the air was cold, sometimes casting frost on the upturned faces of daffodils. She perched in repose, opening and shutting her rust-colored wings, as fragile and undeniable as the faith born again in my chest.

I offered my hand. She deigned to alight on my fingers. I opened the window, the cool morning air breathing life and color into my face. She trembled and then leapt, fluttering into the pale blue light of morning as a gust of wind bore her on its way.

Did you send her to me, Lord? I asked.

Yes, and I will again.

To Read

"Black Rook in Rainy Weather" by Sylvia Plath

To See

"The Incredulity of Saint Thomas" by Caravaggio

To Listen

"Jesus' Blood Never Failed Me Yet" by Gavin Bryars

"Hard to Get" by Rich Mullins

To Ponder

Each of these artworks is about the ambiguities of belief, faith, and doubt. Sylvia Plath tells the story of a "rare and random descent" that reminds her of angels and God's presence even when she least expects or desires it. Caravaggio shows that Christ was more than willing to prove the doubts of Saint Thomas wrong, guiding his hands into the wounds of his post-resurrection body. Rich Mullins rails against God playing "hard to get" while longing for comfort from God's presence.

What has your journey of faith been like? Why do you hold the religious convictions you hold? Are you more like Alyosha or Ivan?

8

Accept love

Self-rejection is the greatest enemy of the spiritual life because it contradicts the sacred voice that calls us the "Beloved." Being the Beloved expresses the core truth of our existence. . . . I kept running around it in large or small circles, always looking for someone or something able to convince me of my Belovedness.

—Henri Nouwen, *Life of the Beloved*

It was Maundy Thursday and I almost didn't go to church.

There had been a fire in my neighbor's garden the previous week. My windows were open at the time, leaving my walls black and my bedsheets reeking with a noxious, unhealthy odor. After overcoming their suspicion that I had somehow thus damaged the whole room with my one small, scented candle, the university provided me with a dark, dusty, windowless room in a Soviet-looking apartment complex near the shoreline to live in while the repairs were completed. It was all very inconvenient. I was elbow deep in an eight-thousand-word essay whose deadline loomed on the other side of Easter, and the extra slog up the steep hill into town made everything seem too much. After dinner, I lay in bed staring at the popcorn-textured ceiling, contemplating whether I really *needed* to go to church. But scruples had their way, and drawn by a mixture of guilt and desire, I resolved to go.

I hesitated long enough to arrive late, and thus scampered into the church at the end of the first hymn. Taking advantage of the muffled cacophony of the shuffling of shoes and groaning of old wood as everyone sat down for the gospel reading, I slid into the only available seat that wouldn't make my arrival conspicuous: the corner on the back row. The readings sped by in a whir, and my mind wandered until Father Ambrose stepped into the center of the congregation, the warm glow of candles illuminating his perfectly round glasses right along with the gold strings of the beautifully embossed gospel book he held. He kissed the book, then calmly announced, "A reading from the Gospel according to John," in his wonderful tenor voice. And then he sang, with his mouth exactly the shape of an egg, the following passage:

> Jesus knew that the Father had put all things under his power, and that he had come from God and was returning to God; so he got up from the meal, took off his outer clothing, and wrapped a towel around his waist. After that, he poured water into a basin and began to wash his disciples' feet, drying them with the towel that was wrapped around him.
>
> He came to Simon Peter, who said to him, "Lord, are you going to wash my feet?"
>
> John 13:3–6

It is the last scene in John's gospel before Jesus' betrayal, trial, and crucifixion. I mulled over the arresting strangeness of the passage. Knowing he was about to be executed, you might think Jesus would do something grand, strategic, impressive. But, no. Knowing God had put all things into His power, knowing all that would come—the suffering, the insults, the pain—He washed their feet. Knowing that one of these would betray Him to His death, one deny Him, the rest scatter at His arrest, He washed their feet. Knowing He would rise again and conquer death, He washed their feet. Their rabbi, master, friend, washed their feet. The long-awaited Messiah washed one hundred and twenty dusty man-toes.

If I were to make up a religion, I thought to myself, *I would not make this up.*

Lost to rumination, I remember almost nothing of the service until an usher gently tapped me on the shoulder.

"He will wash your feet," he whispered almost inaudibly.

I tried not to look horrified, as he gestured down the aisle to a handful of

Knowing that one of these would betray Him to His death, one deny Him, the rest scatter at His arrest, He washed their feet.

people dutifully removing their shoes and socks. It began to dawn on me that it would have been a practical impossibility to wash everyone's feet in an orderly and efficient manner, so only those sitting on the ends of the rows would have the honor. Feeling nothing but remorse for having arrived late and landed myself in that cursed chair, I nodded and started to take off my shoes so the usher would know I understood.

I began unknotting the laces on my H&M canvas shoes, whose once floral patterns were now almost indiscernible after one too many rainy days and muddy walks. I usually wouldn't wear shoes like this to church, but in my rush to arrive I didn't have time to change after a long day of tromping to and from town. I surveyed my mismatched socks with a pang of embarrassment; they were plastered to my feet after a rainstorm earlier in the day. Peeling them off revealed my wrinkled, pink, and puffy feet. And, oh! Oh, they smelled. Biology generally makes us inured to our own stench, so it's a terrible sign if you can smell your *own* feet.

Father Max was doing the washing, Father Ambrose standing stalwartly beside him with fresh water and a towel. Father Max is an old priest, with snow-white hair, a whiskery beard, and wild, ice-blue eyes. He wore a purple stole, whose oversized shoulders jutted out like a suit of armor. He trembles slightly as he walks and speaks, but there is a wiry power in his presence. Mine were the last pair of feet to be washed, and as I beheld the priests' slow journey toward my dark corner of the church, an embarrassed dread reached a low boil in my chest. I hadn't bargained on another human being touching me that evening, and much less touching the most used, tired, dirty part of me.

Finally, it was my turn.

With difficulty, Father Max stooped to his knees as I presented my offensive feet. He tenderly placed my foot in the fresh lukewarm water. It was no symbolic foot washing; he really did wash my feet thoroughly, and dried each toe with the towel, like I was a little child being bundled off to bed after a warm bath. And then, with solemn dignity and unspeakable tenderness, he bent all the way to the ground, his white head shaking, and kissed my feet.

Tears sprang into my eyes, welling up from some deep, untouched chasm in my heart. I didn't know where to look. As Father Max stood, with effort and dignity, a prayer rose in my heart:

Lord, are you going to wash my feet?

All I remember after that is stepping out into the damp spring air and watching as the golden light of evening bathed the broken cobblestones. I thought of the old cathedral, whose broken body had been used to build many homes in the old gray town. It was like Jesus, who loved dearly enough to break His own body.

On my way back, I stopped in the common room of the dorm from which I was temporarily exiled. My friends Aidan and Bruce sat at the large table often used for games in the middle of the room, bent over an iPhone, a half-played board game and two dark bottles between them neglected for whatever they were staring at on the small screen.

"Joy, come here!" said Bruce. "Have you seen what the pope did?"

I peered over his shoulder and saw a news article featuring Pope Francis bent, as Father Max had been, washing the feet of some boulder of a man in a neon-orange prison uniform. Neither Aidan nor Bruce is a Christian. But our conversations are always interesting, usually sincere, and unfailingly refreshing in their frankness.

"That's so tight," proclaimed Aidan with an authoritative finality.

"Did Jesus really do that?" asked Bruce, a genuine curiosity leaking out of his characteristically skeptical grin.

"Yes," I answered, "He did."

"I love that!" said Aidan.

"Me too," I replied.

Twentieth-century rabbi Abraham Joshua Heschel wrote this:

> In every man's life there are moments when there is a lifting of the veil at the horizon of the known, opening a sight of the eternal. Each of us has at least once in his life experienced the momentous reality of God. Each of us has once caught a glimpse of the beauty, peace and power that flow through the souls of those who are devoted to Him. . . . *Faith is faithfulness,* loyalty to an event, loyalty to our response.[1]

That Maundy Thursday is such a moment for me. It is an experience that no matter where I wander, what I doubt, how I fail, I cannot forget. I feel a strange sense of loyalty to that memory, because it was, in the true sense of the word, an apocalypse. While most of us associate that word with zombies and the end of the world, its meaning is much simpler and more beautiful; it is an unveiling, a revelation, a disclosure of things as they really are. As I witnessed Father Max's aged head stoop to kiss my feet, I saw with sudden clarity the fire that burns at the heart of Christianity: that God became man, not to rule, to crush, and to judge, but to gird himself about with a towel, to wash the feet of the disciples He loved, to tell them to love one another, and then to offer himself up to die. His broken body has built the church, and one day the whole cosmos will be the wound from which life springs anew.

Maundy Thursday derives its name from the Latin word *mandatum*, meaning "commandment," the Vulgate's translation of Jesus' words: "A new command I give you: Love one another. As I have loved you, so you must love one another" (John 13:34). The foot-washing service is an ancient service reenacting, since the earliest days of the church, Christ's final night, as the priest washes the feet of the congregation, taking literally Jesus' words: "Now that I, your Lord and Teacher, have washed your feet, you also should wash one another's feet" (John 13:14). And so, all these millennia later, we still do.

It is easy to lose a sense of the strangeness and wonder of this story, living in a world as thoroughly converted (and de-converted) as our own. But it's good to try. God revealing himself in humility and vulnerability is not an obvious, expected thing. In Philippians Paul says that even though Jesus "already existed in the form of God, [He] did not consider equality with God something to be grasped" (2:6 NASB). The gods of Greece and Rome did not wash the feet of their followers; they punished and pillaged and raped. They grasped. They were capricious, and confusing, and unpredictable. But here is God in Christ, stooped, gentle, washing twenty-four dirty feet, telling us to do the same.

I find it hard to believe and really act like God always and truly loves me.

All this, I glimpsed in the bent, white head of Father Max, and I have felt a duty to live in faithfulness to that revelation, in "loyalty to an event" as Heschel would put it. I have not always found this faithfulness easy. Not because it is too wonderful a story to believe; the world is full of all sorts of strange things. And not because it is too hard; all He asks is that we let Him wash us clean. No, I find it difficult because I find it hard to believe and really act like God always and truly loves me. Because I find myself difficult to love sometimes. Because I can't shake the suspicion that nothing is free, that surely, eventually God will get tired of my failing and flailing and give up on me. Because I find it hard to believe He could survey the tardy, wrinkled, and smelly feet of my soul, and bend to kiss them.

Lord, are you going to wash my feet?

On Being an Unlovable Jerk

Stupid. Stupid. Stupid.

The unkind words rattled through my aching head with each stomp up the aptly named "Travelator," a long, steep hill into town. It was late in the stormy days of April, near the end of the first year of my PhD studies. I had moved out of town and daily rued my choice to live at the bottom of the hill I had been exiled to only temporarily the year before.

Flecks of sideways, misty rain spattered the lenses of my glasses, and my heavy breathing cast a cloud of fog across my field of vision. Partially blinded, I put my right foot into a small pool of water gathered where a brick should have been, and I turned my ankle. It was the last straw. I had been fighting off the meltdown, trying very hard not to indulge in the seething maelstrom of emotion gurgling just below the lid of my composure. I felt inconsolably angry. Hot, unbidden tears spilled down my cheeks, already wet with chilled rain. I felt thoroughly miserable. I wished I could be anyone else.

And now, to make it all worse, my socks were wet.

I was having something of an identity crisis, because I had failed, in what felt like an enormous way, at something I was usually good at. Moments like these have a way of unearthing the deep assumptions we hold about ourselves, and that season revealed I found a lot of my value in what I was capable of, what I could *do* and *accomplish,* how very useful I was. Having what felt like a secure aspect of that identity knocked out from under me made me wobble and seek desperately for some alternate means of validation.

We all have maladaptive tendencies, habits we develop to help us cope with life, which are, in fact, not helpful at all. One of mine is an overinflated sense of my capacity to Handle Life. I believe that any and all problems can be solved if I merely think strategically and try hard enough. Unfortunately (for my own soul!), this method generally works because I am a pretty capable person. But this method contains a very distinct and severe downside: if all problems can be solved by the pure magic of your willpower, then all problems are ultimately your own fault. So, I frenetically sought to be useful, helpful, loving, hoping that would shore up my tattered sense of self. Kindness, helpfulness, and competency are good aspirations. But if your worth is tied up in what you do, every action, no matter how simple, becomes an existential threat, evidence for or against your lovability.

So I began to be the main actor in a grim script that played itself out again and again. I would try very hard to be helpful, pleasant, and perfect, only to crumble under the weight of my own pressure; subsequently become very unpleasant, difficult, or inefficient, which led to feeling guilty; and finally return to the first stage of trying very hard to prove I was okay. I persisted in this Sisyphean cycle, descending deeper and deeper into a depressed exhaustion. In all that flurry of effort and exhaustion and self-hate, I was seeking definitive proof that I was okay, loved, acceptable. This love was offered to me in the faces of concerned friends and family, but my poisonous logic made it impossible for me to accept or believe in it. *You can love me when I've proved I'm worth it* was the unconscious argument behind my feverish search for security.

It was very silly, but also very sad.

Not accepting love is like a very stupid existential practical joke on yourself.

If we don't have the question of identity settled by the acceptance of love, the stakes of everything are high. If we feel that our identity, value, and lovability are in question, then in every experience, relationship, and accomplishment we search for the final evidence of our okay-ness. If our sense of self is not rooted and secured in the infinite love of God, we will spend our whole lives tossing relationships, jobs, accomplishments, piety, and personal beauty into an infinite chasm that only the gentleness of God can fill. People aren't people to us; they are validations of our lovability. Jobs aren't jobs; they are proof that we really are useful and worth something. Adulation is a lifeline; every rejection confirms our worst suspicions.

We become like the tiny bird in the children's book *Are You My Mother?* Of each experience, accomplishment, and relationship, we ask, *"Are you the final and ultimate proof of my worth and lovability?"*

To which each activity resolutely replies, *"I am not the final and ultimate proof of your worth and lovability. I am merely*

176

an academic paper/romantic relationship/job opportunity/your mother/brother/best friend."

Not accepting love makes us act like huge jerks, which then becomes a self-fulfilling prophecy about why people shouldn't love us. Although it can feel humble, self-hate is the groveling pride of Uriah Heep; it knows best, better than anyone else, including God. God, the supreme, all-knowing creator and source of life, loves you. If God says you are loveable, darn it, you are loveable! You really don't get to decide. Literally, who do you think you are to doubt God's decision to love you? How high is your opinion of yourself that you think you can tell God that, actually, God has it wrong and should not love you? And what about your friends? Your friends love you. That's their call. To refuse the kindness and generosity that people of their own free will have offered you is not only the height of pride, it is the epitome of ungratefulness.

Ironically, refusing the love of God and others has a tendency to make us intensely self-centered. When you're so wrapped up in thinking about yourself and how unlovable you are, there's no room to think about other people. You don't have the capacity to love people without trying to make them the solution to your deep chasm of loneliness. You're not able to do a job for the pure joy of excellence, because you need it to validate you as a valuable, contributing member of society. The whole world becomes an extension of your need to be validated, seen, loved, approved of. And when the whole world is only as big as your own hurt, it is a very cramped and crabby universe indeed.

I was locked in the cage of my own insecurities. What I needed was love. What I needed was someone to peel off my wet socks and wash my feet. Friends and family offered, in their own ways, and the memory of Father Max was always with me. But love spoke with a different tone that year. We think of love as something soft and warm, like a blanket that encloses us. But sometimes it is as cold and clear as a spring wind, waking us up and straightening our spine. Sometimes love is a rebuke. Perhaps Peter was trying to be humble when he refused Jesus' offer to wash his feet, but Jesus' words were clear in response to Peter in that moment, and they were the words I needed to hear:

"Unless I wash you, you have no part with me" (John 13:8).

Love, the Truest Thing

Let me tell you the truest thing about you: before you did anything useful, or said anything clever, or helped anyone, you were loved. After you failed, or disappointed people, or did something stupid, you were loved. You aren't loved because of qualities that might disappear with age. You aren't even loved on the basis of what you will become someday. You are loved completely, eternally, and right now. Fundamentally, who you are is a beloved child of God. If someone asked, "Who are you?" The truest answer you could give is "I'm a beloved of God."

No one seems to have known this better than the apostle John. Throughout his gospel, he mysteriously refers to "the disciple Jesus loved" doing various things, often seemingly petty: asking who will betray Jesus, receiving Mary as his mother at the foot of the cross, being told about the resurrection, eating breakfast with the resurrected Jesus, bickering with Peter about the future. In the final paragraphs of the gospel, in what feels like a grand reveal, he identifies the gospel itself as the testimony of the "beloved disciple," who is also himself.

The phrase has puzzled many down through the centuries. Why does John refer to himself this way? Didn't Jesus love all his disciples? Perhaps it was because it was not John who wrote the gospel, but some other mysterious disciple. I've heard many pastors hazard a guess that John just liked to lord his belovedness over the other disciples. (He even makes sure to mention that he reached the empty tomb before Saint Peter.)

I am no biblical scholar, but I have my own theory. I think John called himself "the beloved disciple" because his experiences of Jesus caused him to see his belovedness as the most important thing about him. Like Heschel, in his gospel and epistles, John describes the Christian faith not as some set of ideas or theological convictions, but as an experience, an event around which one's whole life is oriented. But in John's case it was not only a "glimpse of the beauty, peace and power" but also the "full[ness] of grace and truth" (John 1:14). I like to imagine that of those many moments, perhaps the washing of their feet stuck out to John as the moment when he really knew Jesus, really understood what it was God meant by becoming flesh and dwelling amongst us. It must have been this moment he had in mind when many years later, as an old man, he wrote these words to a confused and discouraged church:

You are loved completely, eternally, and right now.

This is how God showed his love among us: He sent his one and only Son into the world that we might live through him. *This is love: not that we loved God, but that he loved us* and sent his Son as an atoning sacrifice for our sins. Dear friends, since God so loved us, we also ought to love one another. No one has ever seen God; but if we love one another, God lives in us and his love is made complete in us.

1 John 4:9–12, emphasis mine

This is love. In this passage I hear the echoes of Jesus' words on that fateful night: "A new command I give you: Love one another. As I have loved you, so you must love one another" (John 13:34). In my mind's eye I see the stooped Jesus, washing the feet that would soon run away from Him as He walked alone to the cross, the feet of people who would be fickle and frail, who would bicker with each other and be confused and full of fear. I think in that moment, John saw that God's love is always the first move, and that it will not fail. I think his whole life was lived in faithfulness to that moment of revelation. And after that moment, he was no longer merely "John."

He was "the disciple Jesus loved."

So am I.

And you are too, even if you don't know it yet. That is what it is to be a Christian. To know that you are at the mercy of God's love, which conceived you, and sustains you, and will redeem you. It is not to try even harder than usual not to be a selfish jerk, but to give up on trying to prove you are not one. It means that you are safe in that love. It's settled. That's all there is to it. Nothing, no failure or sorrow, can change that most unalterable fact about you.

I truly believe you cannot be happy in this world until you know you are loved, deep in your soul, all the way down to your dusty, smelly toes, which Jesus would happily wash. That secure love is what enables you to think about other people.

When that question is settled, so is everything else. It is only when we realize that God loves us that we can feel fundamentally and permanently okay, that we are able to fully give ourselves in relationships without losing ourselves, that we can invest ourselves in worthwhile work and enjoy experiences. You can lose and not be lost. You can enjoy things—friendship, romance, work—as gifts when you no longer have to seize them as evidence of your existential value. And it frees you up to be brave. You can try tremendously, because if you fall, it is only into gentle arms.

Don't be fooled: I have wasted much of my life pretending that all this wasn't true. Tangled up in knots of insecurity, and duty, and fear of failure, wringing myself dry to feel like I deserved the kindness of my friends. But if I could have one pleasure in this life, it would be helping someone not wrestle as long with this question as I have. I still go to that sad, lonely place sometimes, still find myself falling into the duck syndrome, paddling furiously underwater to prove my worth while trying to maintain composure on top, but after that Maundy Thursday something really changed. The question of my value was settled, and ever since it's only been a matter of living as if it's true. I am choosing to live my life in loyalty to the moment I understood that Christ would wash my feet. I hope with all my heart that you can do the same.

I almost didn't go to church that night. But there's something wonderful about that.

Because this is love: not that I loved God, but that God loved me first.

And you're just going to have to trust me: God loves you too.

To Read

"Love (III)" by George Herbert

Life of the Beloved by Henri Nouwen

To See

"Jesus Washing Peter's Feet" by Ford Madox Brown

To Listen

"Ubi Caritas" by Joel Clarkson (and me! :))

"Oxygen" by Kings Kaleidoscope

To Ponder

These artworks are about the all-encompassing, never-ending love of God. George Herbert images God inviting him to a dinner that he feels too embarrassed and sinful to join. The "Ubi Caritas," one of the oldest Christian hymns, is traditionally sung at Maundy Thursday foot-washing services and reminds Christians of the fundamental act of love in which Christianity is rooted. Ford Madox Brown shows the indignation humans feel at the idea of God reaching down to show love in humility.

What defines you most: what you do or who loves you? Are you good at accepting love? How would you live differently if you knew and felt that you were profoundly, deeply, and eternally loved?

9

Expect the end of the world

Men . . . propound mathematical theorems in beleaguered cities,
conduct metaphysical arguments in condemned cells, make jokes
on scaffolds, discuss the last new poem while advancing to the
walls of Quebec, and comb their hair at Thermopylae. This is not
panache; it is our nature.

—C. S. Lewis, "Learning in War-Time"

"The world will end in twelve years."

I clicked on the article, wondering who was confident enough
in their assertions to make it into a headline of the BBC website.
I expected one of the usual culprits: a Mayan calendar–crazed
conspiracy theorist with strings hitched up in a galaxy of pins
on a corkboard, or a street preacher claiming that the most recent trendy sin had finally tipped the scales in favor of total destruction of the human race. What I saw was something rather
different. A young US representative, her hair in a ponytail,

with bright-red lipstick and a calm expression adorning her face. She was advocating for urgent action on climate change, prophesying imminent doom if nothing was done.

As I watched her press conference, I was reminded of something we often seem to forget: the world will end. And you don't have to be a religious nut to believe it. It's simply a fact.

When I was a little girl, there was a lucrative literary trend surrounding what we might call "eschatological fiction." Eschatology is the realm of theology concerned with the end of the world, or more precisely the "last things," *éschatos* meaning "last" in Greek and *ology* meaning "study of." In Christianity, this phrase was usually associated with the four "last things": death, judgment, heaven, and hell. In the twentieth century, some rather confident speculations about the book of Revelation gave birth to a Christian literary series devoted to imagining what the end of the world might be like. These books placed a large focus on the "rapture," in which the true believers were zapped up to heaven while everyone else was left to experience desolation.

It ingrained itself in the Christian culture around me to the extent that we were always somewhere between laughing about it and being mildly concerned that it might somehow be true. When I would come downstairs expecting to find my family, who in turn were not there, I would joke to myself that they had been "raptured," and only occasionally would my heart beat a little faster.

You were supposed to want to be raptured, but I always found this unappealing. I wanted Jesus to come back, to make everything beautiful and new again, but I never liked the idea of the end of the world. I liked being alive, I loved my family, I enjoyed walks on our land, and I had dreams of getting married one day and having an apple tree and a bundle of children and writing five or ten novels. Why would I want to be raptured? It all seemed very unnecessary, but I also felt a little bit guilty about it since it seemed like the Christian thing to want. After a few bold predictions were made and missed, I began to feel more comfortable with holding the end of the world loosely. After all, didn't Jesus say no one could know the day or the hour?

As I got older and ventured beyond the Hobbiton of my Christian circles, I began to realize that talk of the end of the world is not merely a religious thing. In its more secular form, I first encountered discourse regarding the end of the world as a competitor in parliamentary debate. It began with the fear of total nuclear annihilation. Not to frighten you, but it actually wouldn't be that hard for all of our globe to be rendered uninhabitable if a few political steps were mismanaged. Then there's climate change. If the doomsday environmentalists are correct, within one generation our little globe could be too hot to handle. Our planet may keep spinning, but what if we can't live on it anymore? And then, of course, there's always the chance that a stray comet could drunkenly swerve into our orbit and blow us up like a Fourth of July firework.

Even if we manage to escape all these fates, the heat death of the universe will almost certainly occur if/when the universe reaches thermodynamic equilibrium (maximum entropy). This is actually the best-case scenario because it isn't likely to happen for several trillion years.

(Why yes, I did just google "How long until heat death of the universe?")

If you really pressed someone—anyone!—most people seem to believe in some kind of end-of-the-world event in which life as we know it is completely destroyed. I find it interesting that these events usually involve some form of judgment. Christians, of course, have an idea of a final judgment. Jesus has His parable of the wheat and the tares growing up next to each other, as a picture of the righteous and the wicked existing next to each other till the end of time, when God will judge truly and justly, and all will be revealed (Matthew 13:24–30).

> **Even if the world doesn't end in my lifetime, I will end. I will die, and all the world will be dead to me.**

This is where we get our word *apocalypse*, which literally means to "uncover" or "reveal." Apocalypse is when we see suddenly who the good guys and the bad guys are. But in a secular understanding, there is judgment and apocalypse too. To destroy life as we know it either through destruction of the planet or irresponsibility with nuclear weapons would be a form of self-imposed judgment, a final and complete failure of humanity's efforts to survive. But perhaps the greatest unveiling is merely this: the material universe is, by its very nature, not eternal. This material universe where we live and breathe and make babies and music will not go on forever. Whether I like it or not, the world will end. And even if it doesn't end in my lifetime, I will end. I will die, and all the world will be dead to me.

Street preachers say it.

Conspiracy theorists confirm it.

But so do elegant representatives wearing red lipstick and speaking calmly.

The World Has Always Been Ending

Why, you might ask, in a book about happiness am I opining about the ultimate destruction of the physical universe? I suppose because I have spent a good deal of my life being anxious about the state of the world. And more than that, wondering how I should live if we really are in dire times. What if our times are the "end times" (whatever that means!)? How do you live when the world is falling apart? What matters? Is it even okay to seek joy and beauty if the worst thing you can imagine happens to the world? It's a pretty big hurdle to happiness. And more than that: it's a challenge to happiness. It asks us whether it is not only possible but also moral to be happy.

I dealt with this in a real way for the first time when I went to Oxford for a semester abroad as a senior in college. The world felt rather shaky then, and I was weak-kneed. It was the summer when the terrorist group ISIL was engaged in a gory campaign of kidnapping journalists, aid workers, and religious minorities and posting gruesome videos of their executions online. There were constant murmurings of random attacks at airports and concerts. The UK was particularly targeted, and so it felt scary to be traveling there, alone, as far as I had ever been from my family. I was so, so excited for Oxford. I had dreamed about it for years, but as I stared at my suitcase packed to the gills with "jumpers" (i.e., sweaters), there was a lump of anxiety in my throat. I slammed the lid shut and tiptoed into my mother's study. I climbed into her large, overstuffed chair like I was a little girl and told her I was scared.

I'm sure she had her own fears for her little nineteen-year-old flying across the ocean. She listened sympathetically, nodding along the way, not adding very much. And then, as if it were an answer to my anxiety, she proposed that we go star watching. There's very little light pollution near where I live in Colorado, and on a clear night, the sky is as freckled with stars as the nose of an Irishman. It was the end of summer, just warm enough to be comfortable and just cool enough to be bracing. We ferried an old quilt and couch pillows out to the front lawn and stretched out on our backs to see what we could see. And oh, there was so much to see! Ursa Major loped magnificently through the sky, a planet could be seen sparkling with red intensity, and a dusting of far-flung stars greeted us. I thought about how the light from stars is thousands of years old by the time it reaches us. It made me feel very small, but secure somehow. No matter what happens to this world of ours, the stars in their fixed dance look down on us, unmoved by our anxieties.

My mama and I talked about the stars, about our fears, about how mysterious and fragile life seemed. We talked about God, and how much more magnificent God must be than we can imagine. When our hearts were all spilled out of their fear, she squeezed my hand and whispered:

"The God who holds the stars holds you."

So I went. And I was very happy, but the anxiety still haunted me. I think my main fear was that something might happen to my family, and it would be difficult to reach them and care for them. It's funny, looking back now I think how perfectly safe I was, all things considered. Compared to the pandemic and its disruption, death, and unrest, that time seems like a panacea of peace. But the uncertainty of the world made me very anxious, and my mind was full of images of the worst things I could imagine happening. How would I go on if they did?

My childhood best friend happened to be studying in London at the time, and so we planned to coordinate our autumn breaks. We had always wanted to go to Ireland, so we splashed out and plotted a weekend trip. It was a comedy of errors getting there. There are four airports near London, and we had somehow managed to buy two tickets with the same airline at the same time but from different airports. It was stressful, but one of us managed to switch. Then there was getting to the airport. We thought we could split a cab, but trekking to the train station at 4 a.m. (our flight was at 6:30 a.m.), we were dismayed to discover there were no cabs in sight. So we wandered around a very sleepy London until we found the only place that was awake: a nightclub pulsating with nondescript dance music, flustered-looking drunk people spilling out the doors into Ubers. An unmarked black car drove up next to us: "Do you need a ride?"

Rebecca and I shared a horrified glance.

"Seems like a good way to die," she muttered under her breath. With raised eyebrows, I agreed, and we scuttled away as fast as we could, our suitcases clattering along the pavement. *I'm so glad my mother doesn't know where I am right now,* I thought.

We managed to get a cab who dropped us off at the airport *fifteen minutes* (I am not exaggerating!) before our flight, and somehow, we made it on. Comically, even though we had arranged to have window seats, our seats were next to a blank wall. Nonetheless, we peered through the gaps in the seats in front of us and watched the sun rise over Dublin.

I was running on adrenaline, fairly sleep-deprived, and hungry. Almost as soon as we landed, I saw a news alert about a

Christian aid worker who had been beheaded. I tried to steel myself. There was no reason to be scared. It had nothing to do with me or Dublin or fall break, but somehow it cast a gray cloud of fear over me. *The world is not safe,* my heart whispered. *How can we live under the haze of fear? What if the worst thing I could imagine came true one day? What would I do? How could I go on?*

I stuffed down the desperate thoughts. We dropped our bags off at the Airbnb and had a scrumptious breakfast at the cafe where James Joyce supposedly wrote some of his most depressing (and thus successful) novels. The day was a blur. We went to a service at Saint Patrick's Cathedral (which we both accidentally slept through), watched street performers, and even had a shepherd's pie in a proper pub bursting with well-fed and slightly grumpy-looking men. We fell into bed that night exhausted. Within minutes I could hear Rebecca's steady, deep breathing and knew she was asleep. I desperately wanted to be asleep. But a vague sense of fear breathed down my neck. My troubled brain kept playing the image of the smiling aid worker who had died. I was troubled by it. By the world, so out of control, so willing to crush even sweet and good people. How are we to live? My mind swam lazily through these waters until I slipped into the unconsciousness of sleep.

The next day we dragged ourselves out of bed, ate a banana and some almond butter, and hopped on the bus to the city center. We were going to tour Trinity College, and then Rebecca had gotten us tickets to one of the best sights of Dublin: the Book of Kells! First, we wandered through the glorious library of Trinity College, wherein resides a bust of the supposed inspiration for Jane Austen's Mr. Darcy: Thomas Langlois Lefroy, an Irish judge. Who would have thought Mr. Darcy to be Irish! Afterward we stood in a long line in a cold courtyard awaiting our chance to see the much-lauded Book of Kells.

They made quite a meal of the exhibition: three rooms devoted to the history of illuminated manuscripts and the perilous survival of this one very special book. Prior to Christianity, Ireland was primarily an oral culture, but with the story of Christ, Saint Patrick also brought the alphabet, and Irish scribes began to write everything down. They wrote accounts of their own myths and legends, they copied manuscripts of the great classical, Christian, and pagan texts, and, perhaps most lovely of all, they made beautiful reproductions of gospels, psalters, and Bibles. They not only copied for functionality but for beauty. The books were intricately painted, weaving animals and plants into leaves, and brightly colored, a beautiful fusion of their cultural heritage and their newfound faith.

The Book of Kells is one of the oldest extant illuminated gospels in Ireland, created between the sixth and ninth centuries. Supposedly, it was begun by Saint Columba (521–597), one of the twelve apostles of Ireland. But what makes it unique is that it survived. It was created during the Viking era, when the "Northerners" would raid and destroy coastal towns. The burgeoning Christian community never really wised up and pushed back; the monasteries never came around to the idea of a warrior monk. And so the monasteries were laid to waste, over and over again. In the exhibit I was shocked to learn that during the period in which the manuscript was made, the monastery was continually attacked and burned, a majority of the monks dying on one occasion. The leather cover to the Book of Kells reflects this perilous history; it is singed with fire, and one of the pages is missing.

I learned all this meandering through the three rooms, waiting for my turn to see the famous book, kept in a dim room where light won't harm it and only a few people can see it at once. Finally, they let Rebecca and me in. I saw it from a distance at first. It wasn't very large, just about a foot long. Under the glass, we could see only one page, but one page was enough. The first thing that struck me was how vivid it was. This book, well over a thousand years old, still shimmered with deep blood reds and bright forest greens. And then there were the intricate designs, animals curled around letters, their tails intertwined, unimaginably detailed. The page was bordered by intricate knotted patterns, inlaid with minuscule patterns of their own, giving the illusion of movement, as though the book is unwinding itself. It was unlike anything I've ever seen.

Perhaps it has always felt like the end of the world.

When our time was up, and we were ushered outside into the biting cold, I didn't feel like speaking. I thought about the monks in their monastery, the Vikings never more than a year away from burning something down. It must have felt like the end of the world, at least the end of their world. I thought about all my fears, all my visions of the worst thing I could imagine happening. The worst had happened to them more than a dozen times in twenty years. And the thing that seemed most important for them to do was to make this beautiful book.

I realized that perhaps it has always felt like the end of the world.

And, somehow, that helped.

Turning Darkness into Light

I have come to expect the end of the world. I think it's only reasonable to do so when all the generations before me have done it too. When I look to the future, I see the manifold ways the world could end, and when I look to the past, I see that the world has always been almost ending. We live, as Lady Galadriel would say, on the edge of a knife. Stray but a little, and well, you know. But this is what it is to be human. Not only do we *feel* like we are on the cusp of destruction. We really are! Oddly, though, accepting this reality has helped me get a handle on my life in several ways.

First, there's a comfort in grappling with the fact that this is just the way the world is. By all accounts, the period of relative domestic stability in which most people reading this book have grown up is a historical anomaly. We might have the mistaken idea that we should wait for a more stable era or season to pursue a good, beautiful life, as if it is inappropriate to live well if the world is falling apart. The opposite is true. The world is always almost ending. But so what? It always has been. Life is lived there, poised at the end of the world. During the early days of World War II, C. S. Lewis gave a sermon to the incoming class at Oxford. The freshmen were in a state of discombobulation, ranging from anxiety over the war to a restlessness to put down their books and pick up a gun. It's a strange thing to study when the world feels like it's ending. But Lewis makes the rather practical point that, to varying degrees, the world has always felt like it was ending. He writes:

> If men had postponed the search for knowledge and beauty until they were secure, the search would never have begun. We

are mistaken when we compare war with "normal life." Life has never been normal. Even those periods which we think most tranquil, like the nineteenth century, turn out, on closer inspection, to be full of crises, alarms, difficulties, emergencies. Plausible reasons have never been lacking for putting off all merely cultural activities until some imminent danger has been averted or some crying injustice put right.[1]

Despite many compelling reasons not to, we do continue to search for knowledge and beauty. The peculiar glory of mankind is that we compose symphonies, have babies, make homes while the world is in turmoil. We are incorrigible! It is not that the problems of our times are not urgent, that they do not deserve valiant and complete effort and attention, but that they are not entirely new. The very condition of being a creature on a blue ball hurtling through space is that our lives are fragile, and our survival is temporary. If the world doesn't end, we do. So when you're muddling through life and tempted to panic because the world seems like it's ending, just remind yourself: nothing has changed. It's always felt this way, to varying degrees. And the world will end one day. That's just the tea.

Facing the finitude of the material universe forces us into a confrontation with our own mortality. Saint Jerome, the fifth-century priest who translated the Bible into Latin, is often depicted in paintings hard at work on his translation of the Bible, papers piled high on the desk, with a human skull precariously perched atop them. The skull reminds Jerome of his mortality, the brevity of his life, encouraging him to work, repent, and love while he still may. Saints throughout the ages followed his example, repeating the phrase *memento mori*, literally translated "remember you have to die." It is easy to forget. Remembering we have to die may seem morose to our modern ears, but it is simply reality. You and I and everyone we've ever met will have to do it. Our days on this earth are limited. Whether we die tomorrow in a car crash, or next year in a nuclear holocaust, or peacefully at a ripe old age surrounded by the people we love, our lives have an end. We have a limited time on the stage of life to eat, work, dance, love, hate, and repent. One of my favorite psalms asks God to "teach us to number our days, that we may present to You a heart of wisdom" (90:12 NASB). Wisdom is found in knowing our limitations. Remember you have to die. But remember also the God who conquers death. Here, we begin to enter into mystery.

To believe in God is to believe that something or someone precedes, undergirds, and outlasts this death-bound material world. To believe in Jesus is to believe that God entered our death-bound material world, commencing an unstoppable process of the redemption of all things. The life that Jesus lived was the opposite of war, death, and destruction. To be a Christian is to live inside that death-pervaded but death-defying story, to live for the light we can see around the corner of the door through which we have not yet passed. And yet that small light illuminates and transforms life on this side of the veil. To me, it is the inner resonance of the Christian life that testifies to its truth. It makes life on this earth better, and if its promises are true, then I am beginning to live a life that will outlast death. To know God is to come into contact with the mystery that will outlast the material universe, and to love God is to brush up against that most fundamental reality of existence.

In the margins of one of the manuscripts found at the monastery of Kells, a monk wrote a poem about his work at the monastery and his beloved cat, Pangur. He describes his cat going about the important business of catching mice and compares it to his own work as a scribe, creating intricate illuminations like those in the Book of Kells. He writes:

> Practice every day has made
> Pangur perfect in his trade;
> I get wisdom day and night
> Turning darkness into light.[2]

In those last two small lines I see why the monks so urgently crafted their beautiful book while the world burned down around them. It was an active response to the evil, a declaration of what was most true about the world. The evil they encountered in the violence of attack unmade their world, bringing chaos where there was order, ugliness where there was beauty. In the pages of those gospels, they saw beauty, hope, and life eternal. And so rather than hiding in fear, or reprising with violence of their own, they embodied the opposite of destruction and evil; they made something beautiful. Something that outlasted death.

This is the work of the Spirit. In the opening chapters of Genesis, the Spirit is described as "hovering" over the face of the deep. In its original language this is a vivid word picture. Hovering could also be translated "brooding" like a mother bird, and "the deep" is pictured as a kind of primordial chaos. God hovers like a mother hen over the great emptiness and chaos, bringing order and beauty through the act of creation. This is God's disposition toward us, and toward our world. Where chaos abounds, God brings order, substance where there was nothingness, relationship where there was loneliness. This is the ongoing work of the Spirit, through whom Christ entered the world. It is this Spirit we bear as we live lives that testify to the love, creativity, and union at the heart of the reality that Death will never ultimately have its way, never have the final word.

And so, we turn darkness into light.

Our response to a world falling apart is to act in the image of the God who made us. We are called to remake what evil has unmade, to reconcile God's world back to God, even as Christ has reconciled us. It sounds like a large task, but Christ has already accomplished it. Our job is only to join the dance, to declare with our souls and lives that death is not the truest thing at the heart of the universe, but life, beauty, joy. The smallest act can be a declaration of God's creative power over the uncreative powers of death and evil.

When you write a poem or paint a picture, you reflect the great artist who will bring beauty out of the brokenness of our world, and reharmonize all the dissonance of this world.

Our response to a world falling apart is to act in the image of the God who made us. We are called to turn darkness into light.

When you go to your therapist, seeking to not let pain or abuse unmake you, you declare that wholeness and closeness is our destiny, not alienation, pain, and selfishness.

When you plant a garden early in the year, removing rocks and weeds, you declare the goodness of this world, the kindness and provision of God that beats in the heart of all living things.

When you work and love and pray, you can do so in defiance of the darkness that would have us believe it is the final word. Perhaps the world will end in twelve years. If it does, I hope it will find you and me living lives that are the opposite of death. Whether that means feasting with our families, or composing poetry, or planting roses, or fighting injustice with all our hearts, or kissing the head of a baby, let us live like love is at the heart of the universe, hovering over the darkness, bringing light and beauty. Like the monk in his small cell, working diligently away on the illuminated manuscript, let us live lives that turn darkness into light.

To Read

"Manifesto: The Mad Farmer Liberation Front"
  by Wendell Berry

To See

Digital images of the Book of Kells in Trinity College, Dublin
Images from the Hubble Space Telescope

To Listen

"Lux Aeterna" by Edward Elgar and arranged by John
  Cameron

To Ponder

These works of art explore what it looks like to live a life that
turns darkness into light. Wendell Berry's poem is a grumpy,
joyful tirade against a world that would invite him to despair.
The images from the Book of Kells portray the artistry of a
community shaped by hope despite dark circumstances.
Elgar's composition (meaning "light eternal") comes from
the Christian prayer for the dead: "Eternal rest grant unto
them, O Lord, and let perpetual light shine upon them." It is
a reminder that though we die, God's eternal light guards
and protects us. This light is embodied in the beauty of the
cosmos, visible through the captivating images captured by
the Hubble Space Telescope.

Have you grappled with your mortality? Ponder the brevity of life and how you would live differently in light of it.
How do you turn darkness into light?

epilogue

Give yourself away

Whoever finds their life will lose it, and whoever loses their life
for my sake will find it.

—Matthew 10:39

In the Scottish town where I live, there is a Cathedral.

Well, actually, it is the ruins of a Cathedral, sacked by an
agitated crowd during the Reformation and left to decay almost
five hundred years ago. But one of the first things I noticed when
I arrived here was that no one calls it "the ruins." They call it
"the Cathedral." This is fitting and right, because it is not fundamentally a ruined place. It is a living presence, a personality,
a guardian. This little town sits on the top of a hill overlooking
the North Sea, and the Cathedral is its crown. All (three) of
the main streets end at the Cathedral. If you stand far away
from town in the yellow fields of flowers in the spring, you can

see its spires, regal and golden in the glow of sunshine. It is the location toward which everything points in this old place.

When I first moved here, I could see the Cathedral from my kitchen window. At first, it made me sad to see it standing there, a testament to its former glory. It's absolutely massive, just a few feet shy of the square footage of Chartres Cathedral. Its gray stones are piled high, resolute against the austere Scottish winters. On the face of the Cathedral, some intricate patterns carved into the stone are still perceptible. I imagine some skilled stonemason, inured to the cold and wind, making his imprint on the world, leaving a little beauty that I enjoy even in its state of ruin.

I've lived under the shadow of the Cathedral for five years. As I finish writing this book, I also close a chapter of my own life. Soon I will move, and the old Giant will no longer watch over me. But as I prepare to venture out, I am conscious of the lesson the Cathedral has taught me. And it's the final word I want to leave with you.

Give yourself away.

After the first weeks here, I began to notice that the houses in St. Andrews all seemed to be wearing the same uniform of resolute gray stone. The uniformity makes the town aesthetically pleasing in a sort of gloomy and stalwart way. The flat I live in now sits on the top two floors of a house built in the sixteenth century. I'm looking right now at our fireplace, in which I can see the original gray stone and mortar that have kept the cold out for four hundred years.

These stones are the Cathedral's. After the Cathedral languished in a state of disrepair for a century, the townspeople began to use the stones of the ruined Cathedral to build homes, churches, and shops. In one sense, it's rather audacious. Can you imagine going to the most beautiful church you could find, knocking it down, and taking its stones to build your own house? But that's what they did.

This town has always felt magical to me, but ever since I learned about the Cathedral stones that make up the majority of the town, I've begun to think that a different word describes it better: blessed.

Since the first churches built after the Diocletian persecution, Christians have blessed the places they worshiped. This is called consecration. To consecrate something is to set it apart as holy and sacred, indelibly marked blessed. In medieval times, a bishop would come, cleanse the sanctuary with holy water, anoint the altar with oil, and pray for the ministry of the church. Crosses are usually affixed or carved into the wall of the church as a reminder that this is a holy place. And the cornerstone of the church is blessed, dedicated to the worship of God.

The stones that were used to build this town were blessed stones.

Those stones, those blessed stones, are the same stones I can see in my fireplace. The Cathedral gave itself up for this little town. Each home in this town was constructed with its blessed stones. I can't help but think this accounts for the blessedness of this place.

As I walk around St. Andrews, I think of Jesus' words, repeated daily around the world: "This is My body, which is broken for you" (see Luke 22:19).

True happiness comes from being like the Cathedral, and like Jesus. It comes from knowing yourself to be blessed, and giving yourself away, so that each person whom you meet carries some of your blessedness in their heart for the rest of their lives. I know it sounds like a truism, something you're supposed to say, but it's really true. You find your life when you lose it. You gain what you are willing to lay down.

True happiness comes from being like the Cathedral, and like Jesus. It comes from knowing yourself to be blessed, and giving yourself away.

Let me tell you about the times when I have been happiest.

When I woke, bleary eyed at 2 a.m. to the round and worried eyes of my niece, Lilian. When I comforted her, and sang her a song, and wrapped her tight in the warmth of a soft blanket and my loving auntie arms.

When I loved someone with my whole heart, and saw him, in moments of glittering glory, as God did: complicated, full of potential, but most of all beloved and bound for glory.

When I poured my whole heart and soul into my silly side project podcast and saw to my shock and delight that it encouraged people.

When I make my mother laugh, and cherish the full, unself-conscious smile across her face.

When I celebrate the successes of my friends, overjoyed to see them flourish and thrive and achieve, becoming all they are made to be.

True happiness is self-forgetfulness. Being so fully who you are that you naturally pour yourself back into the world without worry or self-consciousness. Sometimes this act is richly rewarded with a return of love, a validation of the work you've done, accolades for your accomplishments. But this is only a happy side product of the main event. To get to give yourself away is the real blessing. The true gift is to forget yourself because you are pouring all of who you are into your work, your loved ones, the world, and to discover that, somehow, you are fuller because of it.

The odd thing that I have discovered is that the more I give myself away, the more of me there is to give. It reminds me of Jesus feeding the five thousand. The story is familiar to most of us, but I'll repeat it here anyway. After a crowd comes out to hear Jesus speak, the disciples get worried (as they are wont to do) and tell Jesus that they need to send the crowd away to find something to eat. Jesus frustrates them by saying that *they* should feed the crowd. They object that they only have five loaves of bread and two fish. Jesus takes these, blesses them, breaks them, and sends them across the crowd, and as they continue to pass and break the bread, it does not get smaller but multiplies. Isn't it interesting that Jesus doesn't magically replicate the loaves, zapping five loaves into five thousand? He breaks them. And through being broken and given they multiply.

In my fearful, creaturely moments, I worry that if I keep giving little pieces of myself to the world, someday I'll run out, and there will be no more of me to give. But that is not how God works. When I break myself open, and pour myself out, the love in my heart multiplies and grows. I think this is because when we give ourselves to the world, we are most like God. When we love, we are endless, we touch eternity, we draw on a well of gladness that will never go dry.

One of my favorite passages in Scripture says this:

Have this attitude in yourselves which was also in Christ Jesus, who, as He *already* existed in the form of God, did not consider equality with God something to be grasped, but *emptied Himself.*

Philippians 2:5–7 NASB, emphasis added

Much scholarship has been devoted to figuring out just what it means for Jesus to be emptied, and therefore what it means for us to be emptied. One of my friends helped me understand it. What is described is not an emptying out, but an emptying into. Jesus empties himself into the world, so that it's full of Him. In doing this, Jesus doesn't become less; we become more. We receive the gift of Jesus, of God, poured into us. Love is not becoming less of yourself; it is giving the fullness of yourself to another person. When Jesus does that, He doesn't become emptier. Because He's God, there's an infinite amount of himself to give. In fact, this is what it is to be like God: to empty yourself, to pour yourself into the world through love.

When I break myself open, and pour myself out, the love in my heart multiplies and grows.

When we pour ourselves into the world, we are drawn into Christ's act of self-gift. We don't become smaller, emptier versions of ourselves, but full and strong. United with Christ, we tie our lives into the eternal self-gift of God. And we will never run dry. Do not withhold the gift of yourself from the world. Who you are is a gift. A gift that no one else can give. You are a precious gift to the world, and your aggressive happiness will make this world a place worth living in. Do not deprive the world of the fullness of who God made you to be.

I leave with you this challenge: give yourself away. Empty yourself. Pour yourself into the world.

Pour yourself into the world like a cup of tea, warm, thoughtful, loving, calm, to a planet full of anxiety, ignorance, and coldheartedness.

Pour yourself into the world like a glass of champagne for a world that doesn't know it deserves to be celebrated, delighted in, romanced, enjoyed.

Pour yourself out like a cup of cold water to a thirsty, tired, weary world, a source of purity, sustenance, and refreshment.

Build your life on a rock and be like the Cathedral's stones who bless the world long after its body has been broken. Let the world be a place worth rejoicing in because you are in it.

There is this odd idea that happy people are shallow. It's nonsensical, really, because true happiness comes from loving other people. And love comes from the deepest well in the universe.

notes

Introduction: Decide to live

1. Henry David Thoreau, *Walden*, vol. 1 (Cambridge, MA: Houghton Mifflin, 1854, 1882), 15.
2. The Wailin' Jennys, "You Are Here," track 12, *Bright Morning Stars*, Red House, 2011, MP3.

Chapter 1 Befriend sadness

1. J. R. R. Tolkien, *The Return of the King* (Boston: Houghton Mifflin, 2001, original 1955), 1007.

Chapter 2 Flounder well

1. T. S. Eliot, *The Poems of T. S. Eliot*, vol. 1, ed. Christopher Ricks and Jim McCue (London: Faber and Faber, 2015), 9.
2. www.merriam-webster.com/dictionary/flounder
3. www.merriam-webster.com/dictionary/flounder
4. Dante Alighieri, *The Inferno*, trans. Robin Kirkpatrick (London: Penguin, 2013).
5. Malcolm Guite, "Singing Bowl," *The Singing Bowl* (Norwich: Canterbury Press, 2013).
6. Charles Colson and Nancy Pearcey, *How Now Shall We Live?* (Carol Stream, IL: Tyndale, 1999).
7. Sufjan Stevens, Sufjan's Garden Blog, https://sufjan.com/post/630605891 211853824.

Chapter 3 Remember: you have a body!

1. St. Athanasius, *On the Incarnation*, ed. Penelope Lawson (Yonkers, NY: St. Vladimir's Seminary Press, 1996), 35.

2. St. Augustine, *Confessions*, ed. Henry Chadwick (Oxford: Oxford University Press, 2008), 35.

3. St. Augustine, *Confessions*, 201.

4. Gregory of Nyssa, *On the Soul and the Resurrection*, trans. Catharine P. Roth (Crestwood, NY: St. Vladimir's Seminary Press, 1993), 59.

Chapter 4 Enjoy things unironically

1. C. S. Lewis, *The Four Loves* (San Francisco: HarperOne, 2017, original 1960), 85.

2. Jack Gilbert, "A Brief for the Defense" in *Joy: 100 Poems,* ed. Christian Wiman (New Haven, CT: Yale University Press, 2019), 36.

3. C. S. Lewis, "Learning in War-Time," A sermon preached in the Church of St. Mary the Virgin, Oxford, Autumn 1939, https://bradleyggreen.com/attachments/Lewis.Learning%20in%20War-Time.pdf

4. J. R. R. Tolkien, *The Return of the King* (Boston: Mariner Books, 2012), 211.

5. *The Lord of the Rings: The Return of the King*, directed by Peter Jackson (2003; Burbank, CA: New Line Cinema), www.youtube.com/watch?v=BKIgv8AhffA.

Chapter 5 Tell yourself a good story

1. Eugene Peterson, *Run with the Horses* (Downers Grove, IL: InterVarsity Press, 2009), 39, emphasis mine.

Chapter 6 Be like Mr. Collins

1. *Pride and Prejudice*, directed by Simon Langton, London: BBC, 1995.

2. https://dictionary.cambridge.org/dictionary/english/ambition.

3. *Mamma Mia: Here We Go Again,* directed by Ol Parker, Santa Monica, CA: Playtone, 2018.

4. Rudyard Kipling, "If," *Kipling: Poems,* ed. Peter Washington (London: Everyman's Library, 2007), 117.

Chapter 7 Believe in God

1. T. S. Eliot, "The Hollow Men," *Collected Poems* (New York: Harcourt, Brace, and World, 2021), 82.

2. Malcolm Jones, *Dostoevsky and the Dynamics of Religious Experience* (London: Anthem Press, 2005), 7.

3. C. S. Lewis, *The Weight of Glory And Other Addresses* (New York: HarperCollins, 2001), 141.

4. Jones, *Dostoevsky,* 7.

Chapter 8 Accept love

1. Rabbi Abraham Joshua Heschel, *Man Is Not Alone* (New York: Farrar, Straus and Giroux, 1951, 1979), 165.

Chapter 9 Expect the end of the world

1. C. S. Lewis, *The Weight of Glory and Other Addresses* (Stuttgart: Macmillan, 1980), 22.

2. Anonymous, "The Scholar and His Cat, Pangur Ban," trans. Robin Flower (1881–1946), http://irisharchaeology.ie/2013/10/pangur-ban.

about the author

Joy Marie Clarkson is a doctoral candidate at the Institute for Theology, Imagination, and the Arts at Scotland's ancient University of St. Andrews, where she teaches courses in theology and ethics. She hosts the *Speaking with Joy* podcast, which offers an arsenal of good stories, music, and imagery. She writes regularly for publications such as *Christianity Today*, *Plough*, and the American Bible Society. She coauthored *Girls' Club* with Sally and Sarah Clarkson and wrote the *Girls' Club Experience*, a small-group guide based on the trade book. Joy posts regularly on Instagram and Twitter at @JoynesstheBrave. Learn more at joyclarkson.com.